Royal Jaipur

ISBN: 81-7436-166-9

Photo credits:
Aditya Patankar, Amit Pasricha, Dheeraj
Paul, Karoki Lewis, Roli Books Collection,
Royal Archives Windsor Castle, Sanjay
Singh Badnor, Sondeep Shankar, Subhash
Bhargava, Tarun Chopra

Published in India by
Roli Books in arrangement with
Roli & Janssen BV
M-75 Greater Kailash II (Market)
New Delhi 110 048, India
Phone: 6442271, 6462782
Fax: 6467185, Email: roli@vsnl.com
Website: rolibooks.com

Printed and bound at Singapore

Royal Jaipur

Jyoti Jafa

Lustre Press
Roli Books

WELCOME

Preceding page 1: HUNTING WAS THE FAVOURITE ROYAL PASTIME WITH PRESERVES SET ASIDE FOR IT. THE VANQUISHED BIG CAT WITH ROYALTY STANDING BEFORE IT WAS EMBLEMATIC OF VALOUR
Preceding page 2: THE DURBAR HALL AT CITY PALACE SERVES AS AN INTRODUCTION TO THE GILDED ROYAL ERA
Preceding page 3: THE MAHARAJA'S PRIVATE CHAMBERS DEMONSTRATE THE CUSHIONED OPULENCE OF THE ROYAL STORY
Preceding pages 4-5: JAIPUR CITY, SEEN FROM NAHARGARH FORT, SHOWS ITS URBAN AND CLUTTERED MODERN FACE
Pages 6-7: THIS WELCOME SIGN WAS PUT UP ON THE OCCASION OF THE PRINCE OF WALES' VISIT TO JAIPUR

The late Man Singh II addresses a gathering in the Sabha Niwas, now the City Palace art gallery, while his wife Gayatri Devi sits beside him

Preceding pages 8-9:
Nautch or dance, especially its private performance in ornate halls, was a tell-tale commentary on the royal life: leisure-filled, amazingly moneyed and more than often dedicated to the pursuit of pleasure

Following pages 12-13:
Raj Vilas, the hotel of the Oberoi Group on the outskirts of Jaipur, takes a cue from the fortress architecture of its surroundings

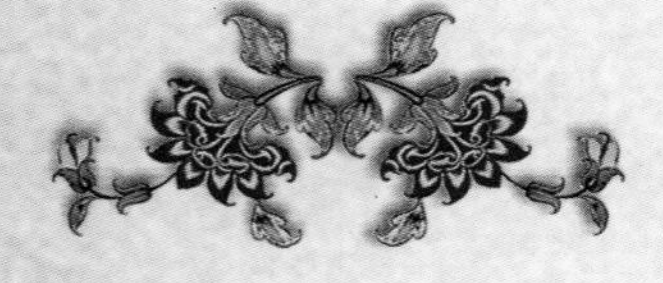

An 1890 photograph of the Sineh Deorah bazaar near Badi Chopar, which along with Choti Chopar was marked out as a marketplace in the original plan of Jaipur

Following page 16: The Amber Fort. Militarily, forts occupied high vantage points and, in an age where attacks from the air were nowhere in the horizon, formed strategic shields behind which a whole city sheltered

Following page 17: The steep climb to the Nahargarh Fort is a simple measure that provides for inaccessibility

chapter 1

Genesis

The Kachwaha Rajputs, proud rulers of Amber and Jaipur, claim descent from epic heroes and incarnations. Their first footstep on the path to power was seizing Amber from its Mina tribals; their long dynastic rule was characterised by adaptability, valour and foresight

UNDERSTANDING THE RAJPUTS AND THEIR FEUDAL society is not easy. Nature nurtured them in a hard school: the stark Thar deserts of Marwar; the harsh Aravalli hills and jungles of Ajmer, Mewar, Dhundhar (Jaipur and Alwar) and Hadoti; the mountain region of Abu. Fortitude, frugality, generosity and a self-imposed, quixotic code of conduct based on valour, justice, chivalry and respect for all—including the enemy—created a unique civilisation. Fiercely independent, individualistic and outspoken, the Rajputs were forced to organise themselves into close-knit blood-brotherhoods, *bhaipas,* to meet expansionist attacks on their medieval kingdoms. Fierce loyalties and easily bruised sensitivities gave rise to equally fierce rivalries, blood feuds and vendettas. Rajput *aan-baan* (pride and dignity) and fighting skills created a warrior aristocracy riven by internal dissensions.

When Rajasthan was still feudal, Jaipur was its most flamboyant and colourful city; its Kachwaha rulers the most glamorous of princes. Thanks to their amazing ability of adapting to historical change, their foresight, and their flair for preserving and publicising their heritage, royal Jaipur endures. For six generations, the Kachwahas of Jaipur took full advantage of the cultural facilities offered by the Mughal court. Styles in interior decoration, dress, architecture, the fine arts and even warfare were influenced by the Mughals with whom they came into close contact due to kinship, mutual trust and travelling with the peripatetic Mughal court. More than any Rajput family, the Kachwahas imbibed the Mughals' 'cosmopolitan' Hindustani ethos. When the British came to India the Kachwahas were equally quick in imbibing European culture.

In the Aryan epics, the Dhundhar region, ruled first from Amber (pronounced Aam-air) and later Jaipur, was called Matsya Desh or Mina Wati. The shortest trade route between North India and the rich port cities of Gujarat and the Malabar was straddled by a town called Amber. The town got its name from a Shiva temple dedicated to Ambika-Ishwara, dating back to the Harappan era (2000 BC). This temple has a sacred tank around a half-submerged stone *shivlinga* (phallic symbol). An old prophecy says that Amber changes hands whenever it is fully submerged.

The Rajputs (literally, sons of kings), a hardy hybrid race consisting of Aryan, Scythian, Parthian, Hun and indigenous tribal stock, trace their lineage to the sun, moon and fire gods plus epic heroes-cum-divine incarnations such as Rama and Krishna. The Rajput clans rose to power only in the seventh and eighth centuries, following the fall of the Gupta and Vardhan empires.

In AD 986, the Kachwaha king of Gwalior in central India, Raja Ishwar Das, turned to religion, renounced his kingdom, and went off to the Himalaya, seeking *nirvana.* His young sons, driven out of their kingdom by their uncle, found refuge in nearby Rajputana. Ishwar Das's son, Soda Rai, attacked and slaughtered the Mina chiefs of Dausa who had given his family shelter when they had been wandering through the wild Aravalli hills between Ajmer and Delhi. In 1006, Soda Rai's son, Dhola Rai—a stunningly handsome prince—married the Ajmer king Raja Ralhan Singh Chauhan's daughter. His dowry included Dhundhar. His romance with another princess inspired the ballad of *Dhola-Maru* and many folk songs.

Dhola Rai expelled the Badd Gujjar Rajputs from Dhundhar and made the Minas allies by guaranteeing their tribal customs, giving them *jagirs* (fiefdoms), and appointing them *kiladars* (fort wardens). For nearly 600 years the Mina headman anointed the Amber Raja by drawing blue blood from his big toe. This tradition was discontinued when the Mughal emperor, Akbar, began a new tradition by applying the saffron and sandalwood *rajtilak* (mark of kingship) on the forehead of the incumbent Kachwaha heir. The Minas also enjoyed the distinction of being the boldest thieves in India. When Raja Kokil Dev set his heart on acquiring the miraculous Narsingh statue from a distant Tamil temple near Madras, and the priests wouldn't part with it at any price, the Amber Raja sent his best thief to steal it. For seven hundred years this purloined statue stood guard at Amber's entrance, till it was

An old view of Jaipur, designed by Vidyadhar Bhattacharya, a Bengali architect, at the behest of Sawai Jai Singh II
Following pages 20-21: Amber Fort rests by the side of a lake that mirrors its span
Following page 22: The Ganesh Pol, gateway to Amber Fort, displays Mughal architecture
Following page 23: A network of galleries atop Ganesh Pol had pierced stone screens for the *zenana*

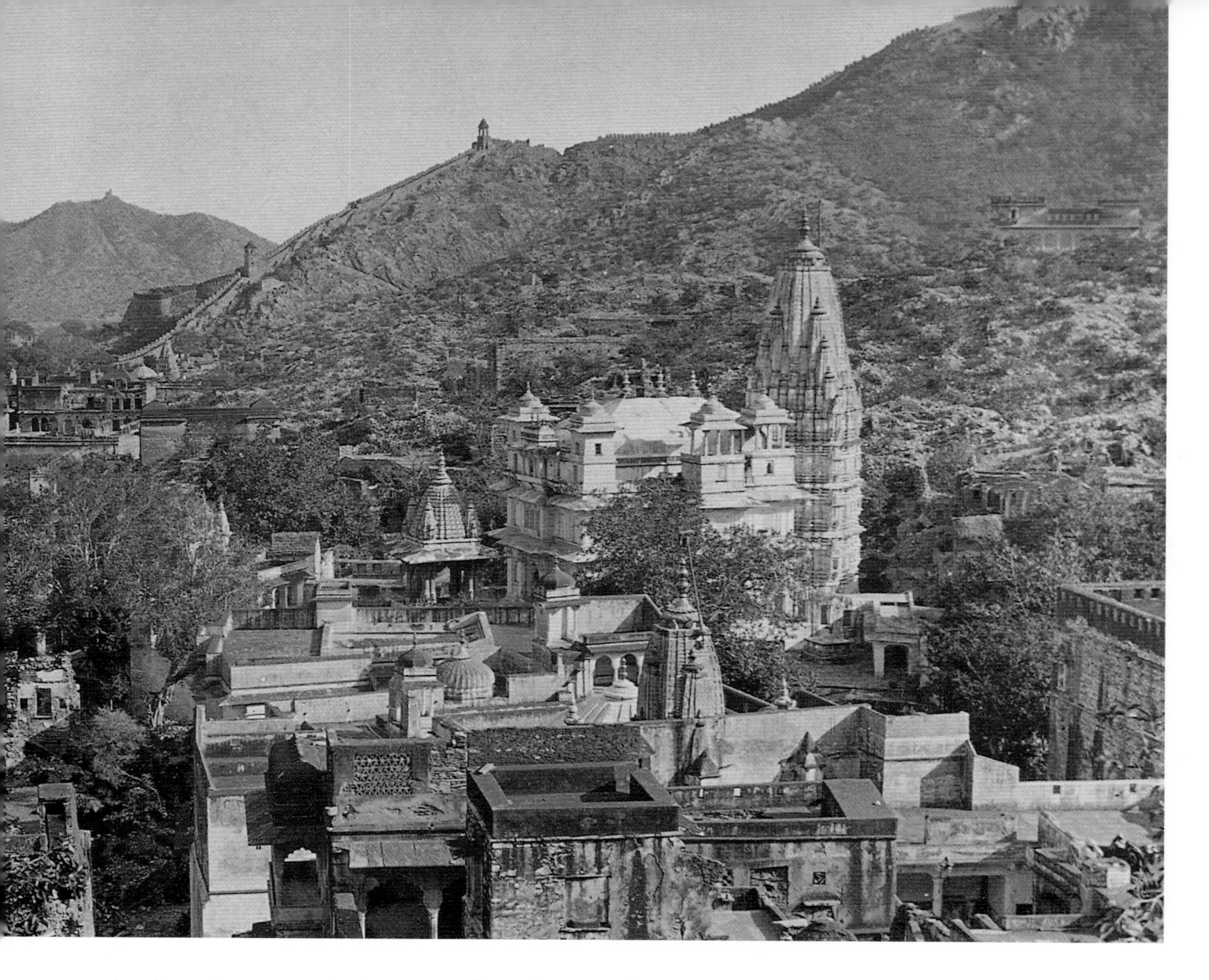

mysteriously stolen yet again in 1948 when the princely states merged with the Indian Republic.

It is said that Kokil Dev took Bairath and the surrounding Mewat region from the descendants of another epic god-king, Krishna. Kokil's son, Pawan Singh, gave the Kachwahas upward mobility by marrying a sister of Prithviraj Chauhan, Delhi's last Hindu overlord. Prithviraj's chronicler, Chand Bardai, lauds Pawan's valour in the long narrative poem, *Prithviraj Raso.* Pawan defeated the last Solanki king of Gujarat and the chief of Bundelkhand in 1182, when they attacked his suzerain. He also fought valiantly alongside Prithviraj Chauhan at Tarain, where, for once, the Rajput confederacy defeated the invading Afghans led by Muhammad of Ghori. A few years later, the Kachwaha prince died fighting a rear-guard battle while helping his brother-in-law, Prithviraj (king of Delhi, Ajmer, Sambhar, Ranthambhor and Bundi), elope with the beautiful princess Sanyogita, daughter of the equally powerful Rathor king of Kanauj, Jaichand. This royal romance had far-reaching historical repercussions for India. But that story belongs to the annals of Marwar and Hadoti (Bundi-Kotah).

Pawan's son, Mal Singh, had six wives, princesses of the Badd Gujjar, Chauhan, Kheechi, Solanki and Devda clans, from whom he had thirty-two sons. According to the laws of primogeniture, which the Rajputs followed, Baloji succeeded to the throne. His younger brother, Bar Singh, founded Barwara, the oldest self-conquered Kachwaha *thikana* (fief) in Jaipur state. Another brother, Udai Karan, became head of the Naruka branch, holding Alwar, Uniara and Lawa.

Baloji's eldest son, Mokul, childless for 20 years, had a son after visiting a Sufi saint, Sheikh Burhan. This boy, Shekhaji, conquered the region that was named after him as Shekhawati. The saint's tomb, six miles from Achrol (on the Delhi-Jaipur highway) still draws seekers of divine favours, and receives royal gifts each year on his *urs* (death anniversary). Shekhaji's grandson, Raj Dev, transferred the Kachwaha capital from Dausa to Amber in the fifteenth century.

chapter 2

Ascent

The House of Amber rose to prominence in the Mughal court through strategic diplomacy: matrimonial alliances were the order of the day, ensuring the survival of the Rajput princes and their subjects and making them the pillars of a centralised Indian empire

IN THE EARLY SIXTEENTH CENTURY, RANA KUMBHA OF Mewar ruled a rich kingdom, and controlled a vast area including present-day Ajmer, Gwalior and Malwa. He also received tributes from other rajas, including the Kachwahas. Raja Prithviraj of Amber supported Rana Sanga at Khanwa on March 17, 1527, but could not prevent his defeat at the hands of Babur, who established Mughal rule in the sub-continent.

Prithviraj's fourth son, Bhar Mal, became the Raja of Amber after a turbulent period when aspiring heirs, often brothers, killed each other, or were deposed by feudal chiefs. This happened despite Prithviraj's efforts to give a share of his kingdom to all his sons by creating the *bara kotri* (twelve noble houses), which became royal Jaipur's premier *thikanas.*

With the coming of the Mughals, Amber's position—always precarious—became even more vulnerable. It stood on major trade and pilgrimage routes, besides being too close to the Muslim seats of power, Delhi and Agra. Despite constant friction with the Delhi Sultanate and the Rajput kingdoms of Mewar and Marwar, which also bordered Ajmer—where Prithviraj Chauhan had allowed the Sufi saint Khwaja Moinuddin Chisti to establish a mosque and a *madrasa*, which became one of India's holiest shrines—these trade routes were kept open by mutual accommodation.When Sher Shah Suri became Delhi's last Afghan ruler by ousting the second Mughal ruler Humayun, Marwar's ruler Maldeo seized four districts of Amber. This motivated Bhar Mal to help Humayun when he returned from exile in Persia with a new army to reconquer Punjab, Delhi, Ajmer and the fertile Doab region between the rivers Ganga and Yamuna.

Far-sighted, shrewd and diplomatic, Bhar Mal also put Humayun's young son and successor, the Mughal emperor Akbar, under a double obligation, first by negotiating the peaceful surrender of Narnol, a key fortress-cum-trade mart in Shekhawati, and then by meeting the emperor half-way while he was on

Kachwaha Rulers of Amber and Jaipur

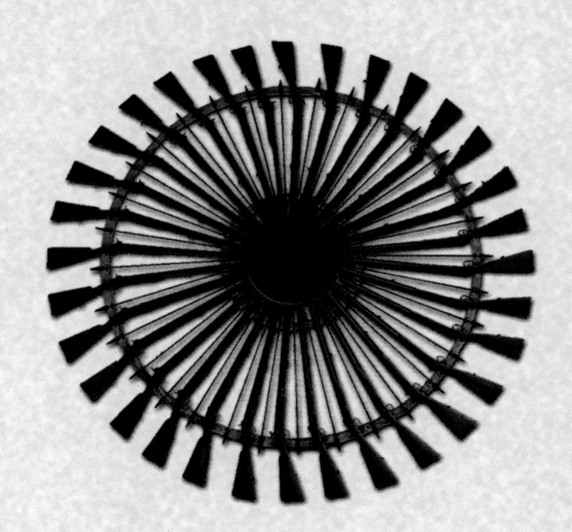

More than any Rajput family, the Kachwahas came in close and often amiable contact with the Mughals. Their dynastic rule, summarised in this chart with the names and terms of reign of its principal characters, was marked by political prudence rather than brash hostility

1
SODH DEV
966 to 1006

2
DULEHA RAI
1006 to 1036

3
KANKIL DEV
1036 to 1038

4
HANU DEV
1039 to 1053

5
JANAD DEV
1053 to 1070

6
PAJWAN DEV
1070 to 1094

7
MELAISI DEV
1094 to 1146

8
BEEJAL DEV
1146 to 1178

9
RAJ DEV
1179 to 1216

10
KHELAN DEV
1216 to 1275

11
KUNTAL DEV
1276 to 1317

12
JOONSI DEV
1317 to 1365

13
UDAI KARAN
1366 to 1388

14
NAR SINGH DEV
1388 to 1427

15
BANBIR
1428 to 1439

16
UDDRA RAM
1439 to 1467

17
CHANDRA SEN
1467 to 1502

18
PRITHVI RAJ
1503 to 1527

19
PURAN MAL
1527 to 1534

20
BHIM
1534 to 1537

21
RATAN SINGH
1537 to 1548

22
ASH KARAN
1548 (Dethroned in 16 days)

23
BHAR MAL
1548 to 1573

24
BHAGWANT DASS
1574 to 1589

25
MAN SINGH I
1590 to 1614

26
BHAO SINGH
1614 to 1621

27
JAI SINGH
1622 to 1667

28
RAM SINGH I
1667 to 1689

29
BISHAN SINGH
1689 to 1700

30
SAWAI JAI SINGH II
1700 to 1743

31
SAWAI ISHWARI SINGH
1743 to 1750

32
SAWAI MADHO SINGH
1751 to 1768

33
SAWAI PRITHVI SINGH
1768 to 1778

34
SAWAI PRATAP SINGH
1778 to 1803

35
SAWAI JAGAT SINGH
1803 to 1818

36
SAWAI JAI SINGH III
1819 to 1835

37
SAWAI RAM SINGH II
1835 to 1879

38
SAWAI MADHO SINGH II
1880 to 1922

39
SAWAI MAN SINGH II
1922 to 1969

40
SAWAI BHAWANI SINGH
1970 -

pilgrimage to Sufi saint Khwaja Moinuddin Chisti's shrine in Ajmer.

Compared to the kingdoms of Mewar, Marwar, Bikaner, Bundi and Jaisalmer, Amber was a small but rich principality which attracted encroachers. Bhar Mal believed that Mughal protection would ensure Amber's integrity and enhance his own status.

Akbar, a truly great visionary and administrative genius, understood that the pluralistic Indian subcontinent could only be ruled successfully with some measure of consent from his Hindu subjects, who were in an overwhelming majority, and not just with the support of his Muslim *amirs* (nobles) and soldiers. The Mughals became Indianised despite their Turkish and Mongol blood, their Persianised ways, and their Arab religion. Since India's Rajput rulers were a powerful segment of the contemporary political class, Akbar needed an alliance with them. When Akbar broached the subject of time-honoured matrimonial alliances between brother princes, Raja Bhar Mal indicated his consent. His daughter Jodhabai married Akbar at Sambhar with befitting pomp and ancient Hindu ceremony on February 6, 1562. Akbar made her Empress of India, permitted her to set up Hindu shrines in every Mughal palace in which they lived, and joined her in celebrating every major Hindu festival.

Jodhabai's role in securing a great measure of security and dignity for the Mughal empire's Hindu population has never been understood or appreciated. By consenting to this marriage, she became the heroic bridge between two cultures, two communities, two ethnic, linguistic and religious groups who learnt the value of co-existence. And reaped the rich rewards of co-habitation and mutual respect.

Bhar Mal's triumphant alliance supposedly shocked most Rajputs who nonetheless lost no time in copying him, giving their daughters in marriage to the Mughal emperor. There were historical precedents for such matrimonial alliances between Hindu and Muslim royal families: the Raja of Ucch's daughter was Sultan Shahbuddin Ghori's wife; the Bhatti princess Neela, married to Salar Rajab, was the mother of Delhi's canal-building sultan, Firozshah Tughluq; a Daulatabad princess married Alauddin Khilji's son. By the time Jodhabai had given birth to Akbar's son, Salim, the Kachwahas had become known throughout India for their political clout.

Akbar's enlightened and liberal policies, his religious tolerance, attracted outstanding Hindus to his court. And his Rajput relations, by marriage, helped him build a remarkably prosperous empire. Raja Bhar Mal, his son Bhagwan Das, and grandson Man Singh were pragmatic statesmen who deserve credit for grabbing available opportunities which turned their insignificant principality into one of the most influential and prosperous Rajput states.

On the other hand, by his stubborn determination to reject Akbar's generous terms, Rana Pratap reduced Mewar's flourishing kingdom to an impoverished, occupied state. His great valour, old-fashioned chivalry and selfless Bhil archers were no match for Man Singh's superior tactics and the ruthless expansionism of the Mughal empire. In exchange for the recognition of Mughal overlordship, Rana Pratap would have gained exemption from attendance at the Mughal court. Also, he would have had to pay only a nominal tribute and enjoyed autonomy, with no forced matrimonial alliance. Bundi's king, Surjan Hara, had already won these terms from Akbar. And ultimately, these were the terms that Pratap's grandson, Karan, had to accept from Akbar's son Jahangir.

Much has been made of Rajput-Mughal marriages. By opting for happy mergers rather than hostile takeovers by the far more powerful and wealthy Mughal emperors, the Rajput princes

A PAINTING FROM THE CITY PALACE MUSEUM WHICH OWES ITS EXISTENCE TO MAN SINGH II
Facing page: A MINIATURE FROM THE CITY PALACE NARRATES A WAR SCENE. THE KACHWAHAS WHO SERVED THE MUGHALS AND COMMANDED THEIR ARMIES WERE ALMOST CONSTANTLY ENGAGED IN WARFARE

ensured their own survival, protected their subjects from the ravages of protracted wars, and became partners in Akbar's creation of a centralised Indian empire. According to the historian Percival Spear, 'Akbar succeeded in giving India the first Muslim dynasty to receive the free allegiance of Hindus as well as Muslims and whose claim to rule was accepted for reasons other than the possession of superior force.' Much of the credit goes to the Kachwahas of Amber and the Rathors of Marwar, whose daughters Jodhabai, Maanbai and Jagat Gossain became empresses of India and matriarchs of the Mughal dynasty, when their sons, grandsons and great-grandsons came to the throne.

By the same token, scions of the Amber house rose to great prominence in the Mughal court. Man Singh, Akbar's ablest troubleshooter, for instance, was recalled to Agra when Prince Salim (the future emperor Jahangir) rebelled openly against his aging father. Such confidence was inspired by martial and diplomatic exploits of great significance. It was Man Singh's victory at Haldighati that had secured for the Emperor the shortest trade and pilgrimage route to the West-Asian markets and Mecca through the Ajmer-Haldighati-Gogunda-Banswara-Ahmedabad route to Surat and other seaports on the Gujarat, Malabar and Konkan coasts.

When some orthodox Muslim *mansabdars* (imperial officials), alienated by Akbar's religious policy, joined the semi-independent Afghans and Pathans in Bengal, Bihar and Orissa, Akbar immediately appointed Man Singh, by then Raja of Amber, as Governor of the *subah* (province). Between 1589 and 1607, Man Singh conquered the eastern provinces and made treaties with various rajas and nawabs for the Mughal emperor. Orissa, especially, yielded rich revenues, having several ruby, emerald and sapphire mines as well as a flourishing sea trade with Burma, China, Siam, Cambodia, Malaya, Java and Sumatra. During his Bengal campaign, Man Singh married two princesses, Shamawati Devi of Cooch Behar, and Prabhawati Bangalan.

It was Man Singh again whom Akbar needed to subdue his rebellious brother Mirza Muhammad Hakim in Kabul. Aware that Hindus considered the ancient taboo against venturing overseas and crossing the river Indus at Attock inviolable, Akbar took a dig at Man Singh, saying:

'Sab bhoomi Gopal ki, tis mey Attock kahan?
Jis key man mey khattak hain, so hi Attock rahan
(The whole world is God's, in which lies the Attock you dread.
He who has an impediment in his own mind will regard
Attock as an insurmountable barrier).

Provoked into proving himself again, Man Singh force-marched his desert-bred troops through the Khyber Pass in a raging snowstorm and occupied Kabul. For four years Man Singh and his father, Bhagwan Das, remained governors of Kabul and Punjab

UNLIKE JAIGARH AND NAHARGARH, THE AMBER FORT WAS NOT A PURELY MILITARY STRONGHOLD AND IT HAS THE MOST LUXURIOUS PALACES AND RESIDENCES. THE FORT STANDS GUARD ATOP THE RUGGED ARAVALLIS THAT ARE REFLECTED IN THE MAOTA LAKE BELOW

Facing page 29: A DEPICTION SHOWS THE RAMPARTS OF JAIGARH FORT IN THE BACKGROUND AND MID-WAY ON THE HILL, THE AMBER FORT

respectively. During this time they recovered much of the booty taken from India by Afghan invaders. These gold coins, pearls and precious stones became the source of Amber's wealth, which increased with every conquest. But the much talked about 'secret Kachwaha treasure' was not the fabulous loot brought home from Kabul, Bengal, Kashmir, Orissa and Khandesh, but the cannon foundry set up at Nahargarh by Bhagwan Das. Cannon casting was a Mughal monopoly till the end of Aurangzeb's reign (1707), and the secrets of artillery manufacture, cannon ball casting, etc., were zealously guarded. Engineers, alchemists and gunners were invariably Muslims who were personally loyal to the Emperor. The main Mughal cannon factory was in Lahore, and when Bhagwan Das lived there as Punjab's governor, he was smart enough to study armament manufacture and set up a similar foundry back home.The Mughals had no clearly defined laws of succession, and Akbar had no rapport with his alcoholic sons, two of whom—Murad and Daniyal—died before reaching the age of thirty. At the time when the succession question was in dispute, the Mughal ladies, the court, the *amirs* and the rajas were split into factions supporting either Akbar's son Salim, or his grandson, Khusro. Preferring to deal with his young and impressionable nephew, Khusro, rather than his headstrong cousin-cum-brother-in-law Salim, Man Singh encouraged family strife and public speculation. But Akbar presented his sword to Salim, who was crowned as Emperor Jahangir.

Bhar Mal's great act of courage, which could have resulted in social and political ostracism—and Jodhabai's cheerful willingness to face the daunting challenge of forging Hindu-Muslim alliance with body, mind and soul—placed a prince of Kachwaha blood on the Mughal throne. Jahangir continued to make good use of his capable cousin, Man Singh; but they were never friends. Man Singh was too independent to please his highly refined and erudite master.

The Amber prince who succeeded in doing that was Man Singh's great-grandson, the aptly named Mirza Raja Jai Singh (1621-1667). He got on famously with all the three Mughal emperors he was destined to serve. Amber's power, wealth and influence increased accordingly. Jai Singh's political sagacity, tact and diplomacy were in striking contrast to the reckless valour and downright bluntness of most Rajputs. Also a favourite of Begum Nurjahan, Jahangir's beloved wife and the real power behind the Mughal throne, Jai Singh accompanied the Mughal court on its incessant travels between Delhi, Agra, Lahore, Kashmir, Kabul, Gwalior, Ajmer, Mandu, Surat and Allahabad, imbibing knowledge and culture. The young Kachwaha prince played a vital role in helping Jahangir and Nurjahan escape from Kabul, where the powerful Mughal general, Mahabat Khan, had been holding them prisoner to ensure the succession of his protege, Prince Perveiz. In the inevitable war of succession after Jahangir's death, Jai Singh remained neutral. When Shah Jahan emerged victorious, the nineteen-year-old Amber Raja promptly joined him at Agra. There, on May 28, 1633, when everyone had fled, Jai Singh saved the future emperor Aurangzeb, from a *musth* (rutting) elephant by spearing it. For this heroic act, Shah Jahan gave Jai Singh the *pargana* (administrative unit) of Chatsu in Ajmer as fief, a gold-caparisoned elephant, a horse from the Mughal stables, a jewelled dagger and a brocade *khilat* (robe of honour).

An accomplished scholar and a diplomat before he was thirty, Jai Singh defeated the Bijapur Sultan's army in 1635 and chased Shahji Bhosale, Shivaji's father, out of Malwa. Jai Singh remained Governor of Deccan from 1644 to 1647.

When Shah Jahan decided to expand the Mughal empire to include his forefathers' patrimony of Balkh, Badakshan, Samarkand, Bukhara and Uzbekistan, he sent an expedition to Central Asia under his inexperienced son, Aurangzeb, and Jai Singh. The expedition was a total disaster because the Afghans, Uzbeks and Mongols rose to the last man, forcing the Mughal army to retreat to

महाराज मानसिंहजी
'प्रथम'

Kabul. But Jai Singh did succeed in negotiating the transfer of the strategic fort and trade mart, Kandahar, for the Mughals when the *mirzas* (noblemen) of Kandahar revolted against the Shah of Persia. But superior Persian logistics, artillery and siege tactics forced the Mughal army to withdraw. Shah Jahan sent his favourite son Dara to perform the military miracle that had eluded Aurangzeb and Jai Singh.

But Dara's discourtesy and bad leadership alienated almost everyone who served him. Jai Singh once quipped, 'Dara has more enemies than Aurangzeb has friends!' It was natural therefore for him to encourage Jaswant Singh of Marwar and other Rajput princes to support Aurangzeb rather than his elder brother Dara on the succession issue. Jai Singh organised Dara's final defeat and capture after Aurangzeb had imprisoned his father and usurped the throne. Aurangzeb rewarded the Amber Raja with a *mansab* (official position in the Mughal bureaucratic hierarchy) of 7,000 horses and the *mahi-martab* (fish and golden orb) insignia of royalty.

In 1664, a Maratha chieftain called Shivaji plundered the rich port of Surat and wounded its governor, Shaista Khan,

Facing page 30: MAN SINGH I WAS AKBAR'S TRUSTED CONFIDANT AND TROUBLESHOOTER

Following page 32: SAWAI JAI SINGH II BECAME THE STEWARD OF JAIPUR'S DESTINY AT 11 WHEN HE BECAME KING

Following page 33: A MINIATURE HAS A ROYAL COUPLE WALKING IN FRONT OF A HEAVILY BEDECKED, MANY-TRUNKED ELEPHANT AND ITS MAHOUT

who happened to be the Emperor's uncle. Shivaji and his followers often raided Gujarat and Malwa, making life difficult for all the Mughal officers in charge of law and order. Jai Singh isolated Shivaji and captured all the forts guarding his hideout, Purandar. Shivaji, forced to negotiate with Jai Singh, compromised, surrendering twenty-three forts and accepted Mughal overlordship.

Despite all he had done for the empire, and the close ties he had with the three emperors, Jai Singh died a sad and lonely man at Burhanpur, far away from Amber. Suspected of aiding Shivaji's escape from confinement in Delhi, he lost his position at the court, and its perquisites. His last letter to Girdhari Lal, Amber's *vakil* (revenue minister), spoke of his four-fold loss: his ascendancy at the Mughal court, his fiefs in Mughal provinces, his personal treasure spent in the Deccan campaigns, and his son's patrimony.

In typical Rajput fashion, Jaswant Singh interceded for his rival's son and persuaded Aurangzeb to put the customary *rajtilak* on Ram Singh's forehead. The confiscated estates were returned and Amber's revenues rose to Rs. 2,50,000 in 1667.

Service in Assam was unpopular but Aurangzeb sent Ram Singh to Assam as viceroy, as a punishment for his father's suspected role in Shivaji's escape. Even though the ninth Sikh guru, Tegh Bahadur, accompanied Ram Singh, performing many miracles to ward off spells cast by Assam's notorious *tantriks* (religious men with occult powers), the Mughal forces suffered reverses. The bridgeless and unfordable Brahmaputra, impenetrable forests, hills, malarial swamps, poisonous insects and wild animals became formidable obstacles. Heavy monsoon rain from March to October made movement difficult for Ram Singh's desert-bred troops. The highly mobile Ahom and Naga armies, and the Darrang queen's navy had the advantage of operating on home ground. Bribed by the Ahom king, even the Mughal *faujdar* (military commander), Rashid Khan, opposed Ram Singh at every step. One day, in sheer desperation, Ram Singh cut his tent ropes, a medieval Rajput signal that the person thus insulted must leave or forfeit his life. Rashid Khan fled to Agra, but had his revenge six years later by having Ram Singh's only son, Kishan, murdered in the Deccan. Khan also made sure that his Afghan kinsmen closed the Khyber Pass when Ram Singh was Governor of Punjab. This infuriated Aurangzeb, who punished the Amber Raja for the Afghan revolt by stripping him of all honours, and banishing him to Kohat, where he died in April, 1688.

Ram Singh's grandson, Bishan, inherited Amber, and was made governor of Mathura to fight Rajaram Jat's revolt. A fearless warrior, he personally mined the Jat forts, and entered Rajaram's stronghold at a gallop when the gates opened to admit supply wagons. The Jats accepted Bishan's terms, but hostility between the Mughals and the oppressed Sikh-Jat-Rajput peasantry continued. Bishan Singh was then sent to help Aurangzeb's favourite son, Shah Alam, quell another revolt in Kabul, where he was shot by an Afghan soldier.

chapter 3

Apotheosis and Decline

Early 18th century was straddled by Sawai Jai Singh, polymath and founder of Jaipur who introduced artillery and matchlock-armed soldiers, and outlived five Mughal emperors. The Amber throne then went to weak heirs, came briefly under the zenana's sway and saw British intervention

THE AMBER *GADDI* (THRONE) PASSED NEXT TO THE MOST outstanding of the Kachwaha princes, Sawai Jai Singh, the founder of Jaipur and Mirza Raja Jai Singh's grandson. From Aurangzeb's death in 1707 to Nadir Shah's sack of Delhi in 1739, Sawai Jai Singh tried to prop up the Mughal rule. Only eleven years old when he became king, Jai Singh was leading armies, planning battles and administering provinces when boys of his age were playing games and doing their lessons. A seasoned warrior by fifteen, he was sent to protect Khandesh from Maratha raids. By the age of eighteen he was governing Malwa, oppressed by Pathans, Pindaris, Marathas and Mughal soldiers who hadn't been paid for months. When Sawai Jai Singh asked for funds, Aurangzeb rudely refused, saying that the Amber Raja had a kingdom, a treasury and a Rajput army to serve the Mughal empire.

Sawai Jai Singh was too young to influence the course of events during the inevitable war of succession that followed Aurangzeb's death. His friends, Prince Bidar Bakht and Azam Shah, were killed, but their brother, Emperor Bahadur Shah, needed him to contain the Sikh and Maratha rebels.

The next Mughal Emperor, Farrukhsiyar, appointed Jai Singh Governor of Malwa in 1713. He repulsed the Marathas every time they tried to cross the Narmada into Mughal territory. Jai Singh also checked the Jat uprising in the Delhi-Mathura region by allotting a *jagir* to Churaman Jat.

Struggles for the Mughal throne intensified. Aurangzeb's successors were too weak and indolent to rule effectively, or control their nobles. The Mughal court was riven by intrigue. Jai Singh, wanting no involvement in court intrigues, left Delhi. It was during the seven years that he spent away from the Mughal court that he began building a new capital.

Jai Singh was, however, recalled and appointed Governor of

Malwa, Gwalior and Bundelkhand, and given the title of Maharaja. But the first Maharaja of Jaipur found it impossible to contain Peshwa Baji Rao, a formidable cavalry leader. The Nizam of Hyderabad, wanting to be independent instead of merely being the Mughal viceroy in South India, allowed the Marathas free passage through Berar and Khandesh, in return for neutrality, and the safety of his own region. Caught between Maratha, Jat and Afghan attacks, Jai Singh advised the Mughal Emperor to negotiate an alliance with Shivaji's grandson, Shahu, and the Rana of Mewar, whose kingdom bordered Gwalior, Malwa and Gujarat.

By the time Jai Singh negotiated a treaty with Mewar, the Maratha confederacy led by the Holkars and Scindias had become too powerful. When Nadir Shah attacked India, Peshwa Baji Rao demanded he be made ruler of Malwa and Gujarat if the Mughal Emperor wanted to save Delhi, Agra and Awadh. Jai Singh advised Mohammad Shah to comply with the Peshwa's demand.

Aware that the Mughal empire was disintegrating, Sawai Jai Singh tried to safeguard his own kingdom through a Mewar alliance. But the balance of power had shifted inexorably away from the Mughal and Rajput imperialists to Maratha and European freebooters.

A matrimonial alliance, unique in Rajput history, sealed the Jaipur-Mewar treaty. The marriage contract between Maharaja Jai Singh and the princess Chandra Kanwar stipulated that her son, regardless of seniority and the law of primogeniture, would inherit Jaipur's throne. Second, the Sisodia princess would be his *patrani* (chief consort), taking precedence over all his other queens. Third, Jai Singh would heed her advice and grant all her requests. Fourth, he would spend every festival night with her. Fifth, on returning from any battle he would go first to her palace. Sixth, her palanquin, elephant, horse or chariot would precede those of all other queens.

A brilliant scholar, astronomer, administrator, mathematician and art patron, Jai Singh was doomed to suffer humiliating defeats and a strife-ridden old age, thanks to the intricacies of feudal alliances involving his female relations. The unprecedented status and power enjoyed by his Sisodia Maharani bred deadly rivalry and strife between his sons and their supporters. His closest kinsmen, the chiefs of Jhalai and Isarda, revolted when Jai Singh's eldest son, Shiv Singh, was found dead one day. They accused the Maharaja of murdering his true heir to make way for his favourite son, Ishwari Singh.

Jai Singh's sister caused an uproar when her husband, Rao Budh Singh of Bundi, refused to accept her son as heir. Holding Jai Singh responsible for this, she attacked her brother with a dagger when he came to reason with her. When her infant son was poisoned, this Kachwaha princess took her revenge on everyone by asking the notorious Marathas for help.

Around the same time, Maharaja Ajit Singh died, and his brother Abhay Singh became king of Marwar. The fact that he was a son-in-law did not prevent Jai Singh from attacking Jodhpur fort when Abhay Singh was fighting his Rathor cousins in Bikaner, inflicting defeat on the Marwar forces, and extracting war indemnity, Maratha style.

To avenge this humiliating treaty, the Marwar prince, Bakhat Singh, attacked Jai Singh's artillery with six hundred Rathor horsemen, and captured and looted the Jaipur Maharaja's camp. In the melee, Jai Singh and Bakhat Singh lost their personal icons of Sitaramji and Girdharji. Since neither prince ate without offering ritual *puja, bhog* and *aarti* (prayers, libation and veneration) to their *istha devatas* (personal deities), both went hungry for five days. News of this forced fast spread to the enemy camp. In true Rajput style, Jai Singh immediately sent back the Rathor prince's statue, enthroned on an elephant. In a reciprocal gesture, the Kachwaha family icon was also chivalrously returned.

This was Sawai Jai Singh's last battle. Having expanded his kingdom and increased his revenue, despite Maratha levies and a drain on his resources due to the Afghan, Jat, and Rajput wars, Sawai Jai Singh was the first Indian prince who switched over from elephants and cavalry to artillery. Recognising the changes needed to keep pace with the new methods of warfare proving successful in Asia and Europe, Jai Singh replaced the obsolete Rajput sword and shield bearers with matchlock-armed foot soldiers.

Outliving five Mughal emperors, Jai Singh turned his new capital into a famous mart for jewellery, gem stones, silverware, copper, brass, marble, horses, camels, saddles and printed cotton textiles. Salt was a state monopoly bringing in huge revenues.

Though the Sisodia marriage promised Jaipur to Jai Singh's younger son, Madho Singh, the chiefs insisted on giving the *gaddi* to the elder son, Ishwari Singh, whom they considered the rightful heir according to Rajput *parampara* (tradition). Madho Singh was only given the areas of Tonk and Toda as *jagir*. The Rana of Mewar—who should have known better—once more invited the Marathas to help settle this family dispute.

Ishwari Singh defeated the invaders led by the Rana of Mewar, Khande Rao Holkar, and the Raja of Kota. Then, Rana Jagat Singh offered Malhar Rao Holkar (who was creating havoc in Central India at that time) Rs. 20,00,000 to put his ten-year-old nephew on the Jaipur throne.

When Ahmad Shah Abdali attacked Lahore on March 12, 1748, Ishwari Singh was summoned to Delhi. He refused to fight the invaders until Muhammad Shah performed the customary *rajtilak*. The Afghans took Sirhind and Multan, cutting Punjab's logistical links with Delhi, while the Mughal Emperor and the Jaipur Maharaja haggled over concessions. Hearing that the Peshwa had attacked Jaipur to install his younger half-brother on the *gaddi,* Ishwari Singh abandoned the Delhi *wazir's* valiant son, Nawab Safdar Jang, to fight Abdali alone, and hurried home to protect his patrimony.

Though the Marathas were bought off, and the Mughal Emperor recognised

THE INIMITABLE SAWAI MADHO SINGH II (1880-1922) VOWED LONDON WITH HIS SILVER JARS OF GANGA WATER WHILE POSTERITY RECKONS WITH THE NUMBER OF CONCUBINES HE KEPT – 41
Following page 36: THE VIEW FROM THE AMBER FORT SHOWS HOW THE HILLS SURROUND IT IN A PROTECTIVE COVER

Ishwari's right to Jaipur and made him the Governor of Agra and Ajmer, Ishwari Singh's despotic behaviour alienated his chiefs and ministers. The murder of the popular *dewan* (prime minister), Keshab Das, led to riots by overtaxed subjects. Revolutionary anti-monarchist men, women and children sang: '*Mantri moto mariyo Khatri Keshab Das/Aab thay chodo Ishra raj karan ki aas.*' (Having murdered the Prime Minister Khatri Keshab Das/Give up all hope of ruling, Galta, where the Kachwaha rulers' last rites were performed.

Considered upright and impartial by his subjects, Madho Singh still failed to protect them from the Marathas. Rajput chivalry and valour were not enough to withstand superb Maratha horsemanship and ruthless guerilla tactics. The Rs. 23,00,000 Maratha subsidy crippled Madho Singh financially, and Jat, Rajput and Pathan uprisings in Jaipur and the surrounding provinces governed by him broke Madho Singh's political power.

The seventy years between Madho Singh's death and Ram Singh II's accession were years of brutal Mughal-Maratha-Rajput wars, feudal uprisings and ugly *zenana* (women's quarter) intrigues. A Chundawat dowager queen became her stepson Prithvi Singh's

Ishwari). Unable to fight public opinion, conciliate his chiefs or bribe the Marathas, Ishwari Singh committed suicide by swallowing poison and having himself bitten by a cobra.

At last, Madho Singh, Jai Singh's only surviving son, became Jaipur's ruler. Despite the feud between their mothers over the succession, young Madho Singh's first act was to honour Ishwari Singh by building a *chattri* (cenotaph) on the spot where he had been cremated in the City Palace garden, instead of at

regent in 1767. The Kachwaha nobles disliked her imperious ways and partiality towards Mewar, her ancestral home. She soon had her stepson murdered so that the throne could pass to her own son, Pratab.

His minority was a bad period for Jaipur. The queen mother had no direct control over the administration or the treasury. The feudal fief-holders increased their own power and prestige by occupying *khas* (directly administered) lands and villages, refused to pay the customary taxes, or to attend the *durbar* (court). The Mughal emperor and the Marathas sent armies to ravage Jaipur, and levied taxes on this hitherto autonomous kingdom. The Jats (another North Indian community) of Bharatpur and Dholpur renounced their feudal ties with Jaipur, and started calling themselves rajas.

On attaining his majority, Pratab Singh defeated the renowned Maratha general, Mahadji Scindia, at Tunga, and started reorganising his state. Despite being at war constantly during his twenty-five-year reign, he built many fine temples and palaces, including Jaipur's famous landmark, the Hawa Mahal. Pratab was a Sanskrit, Persian, and Hindi scholar; a poet, and a great patron of painting, music and dance. He had twelve wives, but his favourite was a dancer called Deedar Bakht. His son and successor, Jagat Singh, was controlled by a concubine called Ras Kapoor, who participated in council meetings, rode out for *shikar* with the Maharaja, and often accompanied him on elephant back. She was known as queen of half of Jaipur, and Jagat's wives had to defer to her as she controlled the *zenana*. But the nobility revolted when Jagat ordered them to give Ras Kapoor the respect and precedence due to his chief queen, saying, '*Raja maney so patrani*' (The king's beloved is chief queen). Unable to fight the *sardars*, united for once, Jagat whisked Ras Kapoor away to Nahargarh to save her life and his throne.

Jagat added to his failures by wooing the beautiful Mewar princess, Krishna, already engaged to Jodhpur's Maharaja. Among Rajputs, betrothal is as binding as marriage. Amir Khan of Tonk, a Pathan chief, took advantage of the feud thus created between the three royal houses of Rajputana to loot Jaipur, Jodhpur and Udaipur. Like so many Rajput sagas, this too ended tragically. Princess Krishna took poison to save her honour and her father's kingdom.

113 years ago, Raja Deen Dayal shot this photograph from the Surya Mandir (temple to the sun). It shows a more herbaceous and open Jaipur, not burdened with population and ecological pressures

By the time Jagat Singh returned to Jaipur, the Macheri *thakur* (nobleman), Pratab Singh, had usurped the Meo and Mewat areas and become the independent Raja of Alwar.

After the battle of Patan, Pratab Singh asked Lord Cornwallis for British officers and troops to help Jaipur against the Marathas, Jats and Pathans. Cornwallis ignored this request because he needed Maratha help against Tipu Sultan of Mysore. Also, the East India

Company was too busy extending its commercial network to care about Rajasthan's desert kingdoms.

However, Lord Wellesley, who carried specific instructions from the directors of the Company and the British government to oust the French from India, believed that the Rajput states could help him destroy the Marathas. He signed a treaty with Jaipur. When Wellesley was recalled, and Cornwallis returned to India, he abandoned Rajputana to Maratha, Pathan and Pindari freebooters. The Marquis of Dalhousie was the first governor-general to recognise Jaipur's strategic and economic value.

Since Jagat Singh had died without an heir, the Jaipur *jagirdars* crowned the Rao of Narwar, Mohan Singh Kachwaha, even though Jagat Singh's Bhatti queen claimed to be pregnant. This claim being accepted by several noblewomen, her son was accepted as the rightful heir on birth. But Jagat Singh's *patrani,* Rathoriji, a Jodhpur princess, refused to recognise her stepson. Jaipur was now controlled and exploited by the *zenani dyodhi* (ladies' quarters) troika consisting of Rajmata Bhatiyaniji, her chief maid and confidante, Roopa Badaran, and her *kamdar* (chief steward), Jhutaram Sarawgi.

The annual tribute to the Mughals, Marathas and British fell into arrears. So, from 1820, the Agent to Governor-General, Sir David Ochterlony, began interfering in Jaipur's affairs, with help from the angry Rathor dowager queen, and senior chiefs like Chomu, Jhalai and Samode. The murder of Rathoriji's *kamdar* inside the *zenani dyodhi* gave the British an excuse to install their own political agent

at Jaipur. In March 1821, according to the terms of the Subsidiary Alliance signed earlier, Captain James Stewart set up the British Residency in what was previously Rajmata Bhatiyaniji's garden.

With her death in 1834, and Jai Singh III's majority, the *zenani dyodhi* realised that its power was threatened. In 1835, Jhutaram stabbed the young prince as he came out of the *zenana* after celebrating the festival of Basant Panchami.

Hearing this horrible story, the Agent rushed to Jaipur from Ajmer. Summoning the important nobles of Chomu, Samode and Achrol, he asked them to take action against their kinsman's murderer. Jhutaram's ill-gotten wealth and property were seized, and gold and jewellery recovered from Roopa Badaran. They were imprisoned and later banished to Sawai Madhopur.

Fatal attacks on English officers and the state of Jaipur's finances brought the agent, Colonel Sutherland, into direct conflict with the Regency Council. Marching into the *zenani dyodhi,* Colonel Sutherland confronted the new queen regent, Jai Singh III's young widow, Chandrawatji. The tussle between the *rawla* (queen's court) and the Residency continued till her son Maharaja Ram Singh II attained full ruling powers in 1846.

A PHOTOGRAPH OF THE NINETEENTH CENTURY TAKEN FROM THE TOP OF THE SANGANER GATE AT JAIPUR SHOWS THE CITY'S TYPICAL AND GRACEFULLY ARCHED ARCHITECTURAL STYLE

chapter 4

Resurgence Under Tutelage

Under British hands, most Rajput rulers imbibed liberal ideas and ushered Jaipur into the modern age. If the colourful Madho Singh had taken ganga jal with him to London in 1902, by 1933 Man Singh's fine polo team had won all three British Open Championships

BY NOW THE MUGHAL EMPIRE HAD COLLAPSED, AND THE British were fighting the Marathas for the control of India, up to the Indus, where the Sikhs and the Afghans were still too powerful to be challenged. At home, Ram Singh found the treasury empty, and the *jagirdars* too powerful. Corruption was encouraged by the dowager queens. Ministers and British Crown agents amassed fortunes while the people suffered.

Ram Singh's tutor, Ladoo Saheb—as Major John Ludlow was called—instilled in him progressive ideas and discipline. A fine sportsman, Ram Singh was fond of learning, art and culture. An outstandingly enlightened ruler by any standards, he brought Jaipur out of the medieval feudal era into the modern world. So, Jaipur was the first Hindu state to prohibit *sati* (immolation over the husband's pyre) and slavery. Ram Singh found that many of his kinsmen and chiefs got into debt by giving huge dowries. In 1847, he passed an edict limiting *daeja* (dowry) and *tyagi* (gifts to priests and bards), and wedding expenditure, in order to prevent female infanticide.

A spiritual man, Ram Singh lived and dressed simply. Known as Rishi Raj (sage king), he had nine wives, but *no* concubines. He would wander incognito among his people, collect first-hand news about their lives, bazaar prices, check on the conduct of state officials and ministers, and their opinion of him. Riding, hawking, kite-flying and photography were his other hobbies.

He built schools, hospitals, dispensaries; Jaipur's famous Maharaja's College came up in 1873; a fine arts college, orphanages, parks, zoos, and an excellent public library-cum-museum named Albert Hall were all set up by him. Fluent in five languages—Hindi, English, Urdu, Sanskrit and Persian—Ram Singh also knew French and German. A playwright who translated Shakespeare, Ben Johnson, Moliére, Racine and Goethe, he built the Ram Prakash Theatre. He was also the foremost supporter of Mayo College, founded at Ajmer in 1872 by the Viceroy, Lord Mayo, to educate Rajputana's princes and aristocrats. He set up civil and criminal courts along British Indian lines. Religious disputes were referred to

Top: An old photograph of the City Palace, with the hills bearing a welcome sign for the Prince of Wales visit
Right: A military contingent marches through Tripolia bazaar in battle dress
Preceding page 40: Sawai Ram Singh II, the photographer prince, during his morning *puja*
Preceding page 41: The seven-storeyed Chandra Mahal, a part of the City Palace, is the residence of the Maharajas even today

a Hindu *pandit,* a Muslim *kazi* and a Jain *acharya* attached to each court. He also set up a municipal committee in 1869.

Ram Singh gave Jaipur railways, post and telegraph services, piped water from the Ramgarh dam, gas lighting and street lights. All city streets were paved, and metalled roads built. Only elephants, camels, horses and carriages were allowed on the main roads. Pedestrians had to use footpaths.

Like all the other Rajput rulers, Ram Singh refused to participate in the 1857 uprising. The British officers and families seeking refuge in Jaipur were treated as state guests, and Ram Singh forbade the slaughter and harassment of European travellers and missionaries in any part of his kingdom. The sepoy brigades at Nasirabad and Neemach, near Ajmer, had mutinied, so the Jaipur Maharaja chivalrously helped the British officers, women and children. For this service to the Empire, Queen Victoria awarded Ram Singh the Kaiser-i-Hind medal and the rich Kot-Kasim district in perpetuity. He was also a Member of the Legislative Council of British India from 1869 to 1875.

When the Prince of Wales visited Jaipur, Ram Singh had the entire city painted pink in his honour. A procession of 100 elephants caparisoned in gold and silver brocade, illumination of all the forts surrounding Jaipur, and fireworks and banquets were arranged. Rambagh's garden pavilion was converted into an English-style guest house for the prince.

Among the Rajputs, adoption is the norm if a maharaja or *jagirdar* has no legitimate male issue. Ram Singh II had adopted Madho Singh from the feudality of Isarda. He proved quite a contrast to Ram Singh. He was not as well educated as his adoptive father. But all his life, this wayward younger son of the Isarda *thakur* (feudal lord) treasured the books he had won as proficiency prizes at school. An imposing figure, with a dramatic fan-shaped beard, powerful chest and arms, huge eyes, bushy eyebrows, thick lips, broad nose, a weakness for *zari* (fine gold and silver thread), embroidered silks and velvets, and fabulous jewels draped around colourful turbans, Madho Singh fitted perfectly into the carefree Edwardian era. His needs could not be satisfied by his five wives and 41 concubines. The *zenani dyodhi* was full of attractive young maids whose sole function was to entertain their master. Contemporaries said Madho Singh was wont to take overdoses of aphrodisiacs concocted out of secret herbal ingredients.

Madho Singh's first wife was Rani Jadunji of Amargarh, a principality in the region that is now Uttar Pradesh. They had been married while he was only a nobleman. From the day he became Maharaja of Jaipur through adoption, this womaniser gave Jadunji the rank, privileges and privy purse of *patrani.* He also insisted on giving the title of Rajmata (queen mother) to his own mother, Rathoriji, only a *jagirdar's* wife according to feudal protocol. Jaipur's dowager queens found this intolerable, and invariably boycotted *zenana* durbars presided over by her. But as long as they lived, Madho Singh gave precedence to his real mother and first wife, building beautiful marble *chattris* at their cremation sites.

Madho Singh had been warned by a sage against having legitimate heirs, telling him that his own son would cause his death. The highly superstitious Maharaja took great care not to impregnate his five wives, who found it doubly insulting and infuriating because his forty-one concubines bore him no less than sixty-six children.

All these royal half-caste bastards were recognised and given the affectionate titles of Laljis and Baijis, allotted *jagirs* (fiefdoms) and annual allowances of five thousand rupees each, a princely sum in those days, even if the daughters' marriages were held in the City Palace *goshala nohra* (cowshed compound), because only royal princesses could be married in the *zenani dyodhi rawlas.*

By the time of Madho Singh's accession, trips to Europe had

become de rigueur for fashionable Maharajas and other pillars of the British empire. Madho Singh attended King Edward VII's coronation in 1902 in his inimitable style. At the head of his cavalcade rode the bejewelled family icons of Sitaramji. Crowds gathered to gape at the colourful Maharaja whenever he went shopping or attended banquets.

Edward VII entertained him at Windsor Castle, reciprocating Ram Singh II's hospitality. Victoria's jovial successor also insisted on seeing 'those colossal holy water jugs all London is talking about!' Madho Singh had carried a supply of *ganga jal* (holy water from the river Ganges) for his daily *puja* (prayers) in two enormous silver containers, the largest silver artifacts in existence.

Madho Singh was famous for his generosity and humour. Once he asked the plump, rosy-cheeked Chauth Mal, his royal taster, 'What do you eat that keeps you so healthy?' Mal promptly replied, 'Your food, before you.' In London, Chauth Mal narrowly escaped being turned into a prizefighter by Lord Crawford, who wrestled with him once, and asked the Maharaja to loan him this potential winner. Reluctant to part with his taster, or refuse a guest, Madho Singh ordered an identification parade on the plea that he didn't know which of his two hundred-odd servants was wanted. They all turned up covered in wheat flour! Unable to recognise Chauth Mal, Crawford departed. Madho Singh rewarded Chauth Mal with the biggest box of chocolates Fortnum and Mason could deliver.

Madho Singh had two other favourites—his valet Bala Bux Khwas, and a dancing girl, Roop Rai. They were determined to squeeze every advantage from the deteriorating and heirless Maharaja, and even hit upon a plan to isolate him from the British Resident, Jaipur's council of ministers and nobles, who might curtail their hold over him.

When Madho Singh needed an heir he naturally looked towards Isarda. When his grand-nephew, Mor Mukat, became Sawai Man Singh II, he often said, 'I became Maharaja of Jaipur by *bhagwati kripa* (God's grace). Otherwise I wouldn't even have become *thakur* of Isarda.' Destiny certainly had something to do with this out-of-turn elevation, because Madho Singh had twenty-nine natural sons. Because of the prediction that he would die the day he had a legitimate heir, he kept the name of his chosen successor a secret even on his deathbed.

Several months earlier, Madho Singh had called his grand-nephews, Bahadur and Mor Mukat, to the City Palace. Both boys offered the customary gold coin as *nazar* (tribute) to their Maharaja. Since he was busy talking to someone else, Mor Mukat put the coin into his pocket and sat down, while his elder brother kept standing according to protocol. Observing the younger boy's independence of spirit and *sang froid,* Maharaja Madho Singh moved him into the City Palace with the obvious intention of adopting him.

Ugly intrigues and bitter tussles over who should inherit Jaipur began. Eyewitnesses swore there were attempts on the ten-year-old heir presumptive's life. Mor Mukat's paternal aunts were married to the Maharao of Kotah, and to his cousin-cum-*dewan*, Aapji Saheb of Palaitha. Therefore it was natural for the shrewd *thakur* of Isarda to send his son off to Kotah, where he would be secure under the double protection of his powerful relations.

Two adoptions in a row from Isarda were as unacceptable to the Jaipur nobility as to the British. The *thakur* of Jhalai got twenty-five *tazimi sardars* (hereditary peers), including Chomu and Diggi, to sign a note of protest addressed to the Viceroy, Lord Chelmsford. Ganga Singh, Maharaja of Bikaner, told the Viceroy that Jhalai, the senior-most branch of the royal Kachwahas, had first claim on Jaipur's throne. Bikaner's arch-enemy, Alwar's reactionary Maharaja Jai Singh, countered this by informing the viceroy that according to Rajput *parampara* the Maharaja of Jaipur was free to adopt a boy from Isarda, Jhalai, Barwara or Uniara—the Raja of Bikaner was advocating Jhalai's case only because the boy was his nephew.

The fact that Maharaja Ganga Singh and Madho Singh were married to two Tanwar sisters added a piquant twist to the adoption imbroglio. The Kachwaha clan on the whole detested this Rathor interference in their internal affairs, especially since Sir Pratab—Jodhpur's influential regent and virtual leader of India's seventeen Rathor kingdoms—took full advantage of this situation by negotiating not one, but two matrimonial alliances for his nieces. It was only after the Isarda boy accepted the coconuts sent by way of betrothal pledges to the much older and plain Princess Marudhar Kanwar, and Princess Kishore Kanwar (mercifully pretty and four years younger than her fiance), that Mor Mukat's adoption received the Viceroy's official seal, and the King-Emperor's blessings.

But the Jaipur heir-apparent's adventures continued. Aware that their benefactor Madho Singh's days were numbered, Bala Bux

Khwas and Roop Rai took the Maharaja and his adopted son off to Sawai Madhopur on the pretext of *shikar* (hunt). This alarmed the British government because he was very sick and could easily be coerced into signing away his heritage to unscrupulous favourites. The Agent instructed the Resident, Patterson, to escort Madho Singh back to his capital so he could die in a manner befitting his station, and to take young Mor Mukut Singh into protective custody.

In 1922, Mor Mukut became Sawai Man Singh II of Jaipur. A regency council consisting of the Resident and premier *jagirdars* was set up. In his official will Maharaja Madho Singh had appointed his personal physician, Sir James Roberts, and his brother-in-law, Thakur Bhairon Singh Tanwar, as his heir's joint guardians. The Viceroy appointed Colonel Twiss, J.W.C. Mayne and Thakur Dhonkal Singh as tutors to the boy-king.

Despite great opposition from the dowager queens and the chiefs who sat on the Regency Council, Sir James and the Resident moved the twelve-year-old Maharaja to Rambagh, away from insidious *zenana* influences and the City Palace's intrigue-ridden environment. The fear of poisoning or 'accidental' death was real, for there were many rival claimants for Jaipur's rich *gaddi.*

A private school was started for the Maharaja, his elder brother, Bahadur, and several cousins, by the English doctor, Sir James. But it soon proved inadequate. Riding and horseplay took precedence over the three 'Rs.'

For once, the Resident, the Regency Council, the English and Indian guardians and the dowager queens agreed on something. The Maharaja needed better discipline and education than he was getting in the luxurious ambience of Rambagh Palace. Ram Singh's widow, Dadiji Shri Rathoriji—as tough-minded and sharp-tongued as her nephew, Sir Pratab—summoned the Resident and ordered him to remove Man Singh from Jaipur before his mind and body were damaged. The young Jaipur Maharaja was sent to India's Eton, Mayo College, only eighty miles away at Ajmer.

Back home the Regency Council did some excellent work. In 1927, when most small towns and villages were not electrified, electricity came to Jaipur's townships. Budgeting and auditing of accounts were introduced by the new Revenue Secretary, an officer of the Indian Civil Service, on loan from the British Indian government. The Council also appointed a new Law Officer, modernised the police force, and discontinued the practice established since the days of Jai Singh II, of shutting the city's gates at night, which though necessary at one time for purposes of security, was a source of great annoyance and hardship during the more settled circumstances of the twentieth century. The throwing open of these gates marked a new era in the history of royal Jaipur. The feudal levy on the horses and soldiers of the chiefs was also abolished to make way for cash tributes, which were determined by the size and revenue of each fiefdom.

Jaipur's revenues came from the Sambhar salt lakes, agricultural tax on landlords, factory and shop licenses, railway revenue, custom and excise duties, levies on stone quarrying and forest produce, copper and emerald mines, tolls on road use, and charges on water and electricity. There was no income tax, and all farmers could graze their livestock on state land, free of charge. Since Ram Singh's time, only one-eighth of the revenues went to the royal household, the rest went to the state exchequer, and was used to pay salaries to public servants, and to construct and maintain public works.

Man Singh II was not an intellectual or a great political reformer. By inclination he was a sportsman and a soldier. Charming, good looking and extremely affable, he was unruffled by the tumult and the theatrics which surrounded him during his childhood. In 1923, he married the senior Jodhpur princess. First Her Highness, as she was always called, became the mother of Princess Prem Kanwar or Micky, and Maharaj Kumar Bhawani Singh or Bubbles (so named on account of the prodigious quantities of champagne consumed on his birth). The younger princess of Jodhpur was married to him at the age of fourteen in 1932. Maharaj Kumar Jai Singh and Prithviraj Singh, or Joe and Pat, are the sons of Second Her Highness.

This dual relationship brought Man Singh into close contact with Jodhpur's fascinating regent, Sir Pratab. The best polo players came from a Jodhpur family—the Jodha Rathors of Marwar. H.H. the Maharaja of Jaipur talked Sir Pratab into parting with the best-trained polo ponies in India. According to Rajput custom, sons-in-law had to be appeased at any cost!

Polo became the focal point of Man Singh's life. Every year he went to Calcutta, Delhi and Bombay for the winter season, and to England in summer. By 1933, Man Singh had one of the finest polo teams in the world, consisting of himself, Maharaj Prithi Singh of Baria, and Rao Rajas Hanaut and Abhey, natural sons of Sir Pratab.

MAHARANI GAYATRI DEVI WITH HER HUSBAND MAN SINGH II DURING A PUBLIC FUNCTION. INTEREST IN THE GAME OF POLO WAS A PERCURSOR TO THEIR PLAYING THE GAME OF LOVE

Facing page 46: MAN SINGH II (1922-1969) WAS A KEEN POLO PLAYER AND KEENER ADVOCATE OF MODERNITY

Born horsemen, they bought and trained their own ponies, mostly Australian thoroughbreds crossed with Marwari and Kathiawari horses to give stamina, speed and that extra responsiveness so essential in a good polo horse. Combined with the tenacity and the derring-do of the Rajput this was a winning combination. In the same year, the Jaipur team made polo history by winning all three British Open Championships—the King's Coronation Cup at Hurlingham, the Rugby Challenge Cup and the Open Senior Cup at Dunster. Earlier, it had won the Hurlingham and Roehampton championships. The select polo world, dominated by Britain, America and Argentina, opened to admit the dashing Indian raja.

A shared interest in riding and European travel brought Man Singh and Princess Ayesha together. Ayesha's mother, the daughter of the progressive Maharaja of Baroda, Sayaji Rao Gaekwad, was the Maharani of Cooch Behar. During the polo season, this superb horsewoman and hostess entertained the Jaipur Maharaja as a house guest. It was natural for Man Singh to take her children Bhaiya (the Maharaja of Cooch Behar), Ila, Menaka, Ayesha (Gayatri Devi) and Inderjeet Singh for treats. What started as a family friendship between the twenty-six-year-old Jaipur Maharaja and the fourteen-year-old Ayesha turned into a six-year courtship.

Celebrating a Princess

Gayatri Devi, 82, is still the finest face of royalty in India. She has played a succession of public roles with quiet grace, gentility and world-winning charm

Once identified by Vogue as one of the ten most beautiful women in the world, she was born in London and had the best of the East and West for her education - going to Santiniketan and to a science school in Switzerland among others.

Her love story and subsequent marriage to Man Singh II was the stuff that fairy tales are made of. Third wife of the latter, it was their love for polo that brought them together. Marriage saw her assume a variety of roles with equal finesse: a Captain's wife when her husband fought during WW II; a canvassing politician who won by the largest majority ever as recorded in the Guinness Book of World Records; and wife of the Indian ambassador to Spain.

Widowed suddenly in 1970, she took over the mantle as Rajmata of Jaipur.

Maharaja Man Singh II at Ramgarh with guests and personal staff and the first tiger he had slain

Facing page 51: In the December of 1947, the silver jubilee of Man Singh II's accession to the throne was held. Standing outside the Chinese room in Rambagh Palace are: (in the first row, second from left) Pamela Mountbatten, (fourth from left) Lord and Lady Mountbatten, (sixth from left) Maharaja Man Singh II

Though extremely fond of Man Singh, the dowager queen of Cooch Behar didn't want her stunningly beautiful and brilliant daughter to became anyone's third wife. Ayesha was withdrawn from Rabindranath Tagore's school in Santiniketan, and sent to study in England. The Jaipur Maharaja followed her there.

By the time she was seventeen, Man Singh had asked her to become his wife. Though she agreed happily, her family disapproved. They felt that she could never hope for a paramount position in Jaipur, or become the mother of future kings because Man Singh's contemplated marriage provoked hostility in Rajasthan and official British circles for fear of future complications. Aware of all this, the most cosmopolitan royal clique of this era—the Barodas and the Cooch Behars—thought it best to remove Ayesha from Man Singh's orbit. But in 1940, the dowager queen relented, and Man Singh married Princess Ayesha in a traditional ceremony. Ayesha became Maharani Gayatri Devi of Jaipur.

In Rambagh Palace, all the queens had their own apartments, kitchens, gardens, household staff and cars. The two Jodhpur princesses observed *purdah,* but Gayatri Devi rode with the Maharaja (or his elder brother) every morning, and swam and breakfasted with him in the poolside garden. They played tennis, badminton or squash in the evenings, and went on *shikar* camps during the hunting season.

First Her Highness had the highest status as mother of Jaipur's first direct heir in nearly a century. It was she who controlled the *zenani dyodhi's* four hundred-odd inmates, occupied the *bada rawla* (chief queen's court) and dispensed pensions and financial help to retainers, poor relations and other subjects who approached her. Religious functions were also conducted under her direction. She took precedence over her niece, Kishore Kanwar, and Gayatri Devi.

Second Her Highness was warm and vivacious, and a generous hostess with the inherent aplomb of the Jodhpur royal family. Well-read, well-versed in Indian and western classical music, and widely travelled, she had a penchant for chain-smoking, iced cocktails and impromptu parties. She was nevertheless no match for her husband's third wife. She might have enjoyed greater power and privilege after First Her Highness's death—taking care of all the children, holding the *toshakhana* (royal treasury) keys, enjoying long racing holidays in England, Ooty, Bombay and Bangalore, and entertaining dignitaries, but she played a diminishing role in her husband's life and home with the arrival of Gayatri Devi.

Man Singh believed that Gayatri Devi's progressive example would encourage other women to emulate her. But even the highest officials and aristocrats continued to leave their wives home when they were invited to Rambagh Palace.

Gayatri Devi realised that the only way to modernise Rajasthani society was through education. The daughters of the nobility lived in secluded forts and *havelis* (mansions), received little education and were married off in their early teens. There were some convent schools in Rajasthan, but orthodox Hindu parents were loath to send their daughters there, fearing unwelcome religious influences. To fill the gap, Gayatri Devi opened a school for girls in 1942, that was to become the best of its kind in all Asia.

Gayatri Devi had the support of a truly progressive and far-sighted husband. Much of modern Jaipur—the present Rajasthan State Assembly, the Maharaja's and Maharani's colleges, the Rajasthan University buildings, the Ashok Club, the Flying Club and the Civil Lines—were all Man Singh's creation. In 1942, he brought Mirza Ismail, the architect of modern Mysore and Bangalore, to Jaipur as his *dewan* (prime minister).

chapter 5

Coup de Grace

The merger of the princely states with the Indian Union robbed them of much of their shine. Whatever rights they were holding on to were taken away by the 1971 amendment to the Constitution. Yet Jaipur rulers entered political life and embarked on their careers

ROYALTY SITS TOGETHER. THE OLDER PRINCE IS IN A ROUND-COLLAR SUIT AND THE UBIQUITOUS TURBAN; THE CHILDREN ARE NOT SO ENCUMBERED

Facing page 52: BHAWANI SINGH, THE PRESENT MAHARAJA, HAD A CAREER IN THE ARMY AND IS NOW A HOTELIER

BY 1946, IT WAS CLEAR THAT THE PRINCELY STATES MUST adapt to a changing world. The spirit of democracy was abroad, and Jaipur got an elected legislative assembly. Maharaja Sadul Singh of Bikaner—then president of the Chamber of Princes—convinced most princes to join the Indian federation because it was unrealistic to think of forming a separate bloc consisting of 517 princely states. But they all wanted a united, independent India, opposing Partition to the very end in all their missives to British and Indian leaders.

The States Department and India's first Home Minister, Vallabhbhai Patel, sent a civil servant, V.P. Menon, to negotiate accession and merger treaties with the princely states. Sardar Patel assured the princes that their autonomy would be respected if they acceded in three areas—defence, foreign affairs and communications. But the Viceroy's political secretary, Corfield, who had been Resident at Jaipur and other states, warned them that they would be signing their own class into oblivion if they did not insist on iron-clad constitutional guarantees on their powers, privileges and privy purses. The princes refused to sign. Mountbatten dismissed Corfield and began negotiations personally.

The Chamber of Princes met at Delhi on July 25, 1947. The Viceroy assured them that the government would stand by them, and that they wouldn't be signing away any rights, especially since the concessions they were making had already been made in 1857 to the paramount power, Great Britain, and would merely pass on to its successor, the government of independent India. Turning down Jinnah's offer of unconditional autonomy in return for joining

Pakistan, the four largest Rajput states—Jodhpur, Jaisalmer, Bikaner and Jaipur—opted for secular India.

In December 1947, the silver jubilee of Man Singh's reign was celebrated with great pomp. Mountbatten, now Governor-General of independent India, and his wife Edwina, were the chief guests.

But for sheer extravagance, his only daughter Princess Prem Kanwar's marriage to Prince Jaideep Singh of Baria made it to the Guinness Book. There were 800 guests from several princely families. Those who were there still recall the grand processions, banquets and entertainment programmes; the rich trousseau from the best shops in India and Europe, and the bride's fabulous jewellery. No wonder, for she was the first legitimate daughter to be given in marriage by a Jaipur Maharaja in nearly 200 years!

The merger of the princely states with a socialist democracy affected every royal family. Jaipur, however, had advantages that helped its selection as the capital of Rajasthan. Its extremely popular and capable Maharaja was appointed *raj pramukh* of the state.

Man Singh's first duty as *raj pramukh* was to preside over the disbandment of his state forces. Only the Sawai Man Singh Guards—with whom he had served in the northern frontier during the Second World War—retained its identity after being incorporated into the Indian Army. The Kachwaha Horse and other cavalry regiments were amalgamated into the 61st Cavalry, India's only mounted regiment. It provides the president's bodyguard with its ceremonial horse squadrons.

H.H. Jaipur's privy purse was fixed at Rs. 22,00,000. This in no way compensated for the cash reserves handed over, along with the sixteen thousand square miles of territory, railway lines and rolling stock worth crores (millions) of rupees, innumerable public works, and intangible human assets.

Apart from maintaining themselves in luxury, maharajas also used their privy purses to support hundreds of relations, retainers and dependents who could not suddenly be turned out to fend for themselves. Historic forts, palaces and temples had to be maintained without state revenue. Religious festivals and public ceremonies which the people expected their maharajas to perform—and visitors flocked to see—also cost money.

When the *raj pramukh's* post was abolished, Man Singh emulated British aristocrats like the Duke of Bedford and Lord Bath by turning his stately home, Rambagh, into a palace hotel. His only surviving wife, Maharani Gayatri Devi, moved into the much smaller Raj Mahal, the former Residency.

Man Singh kept in step with changing times, sending his three sons out to work as soon as they were out of Harrow. His heir Bubbles joined the Indian Army, became Adjutant, and finally

After returning from the silver jubilee ceremony of his accession, Man Singh and Lord and Lady Mountbatten pose for a photograph

Facing page 55: The Maharaja with the first Home Minister of independent India, Sardar Vallabhbhai Patel, at the March 13, 1949 oath-taking ceremony for the *Raj Pramukh* of Rajasthan

Commandant of the President's Body Guard. In 1966, he married Padmini, the princess of Sirmor. This matrimonial alliance was contracted by Man Singh in typical Rajput fashion to redeem a pledge made earlier to the Raja of Sirmor.

Joe joined the Rothschild banking firm, gaining first-hand knowledge and experience which came in handy in dealing with the Jaipur family's countless assets and investments. Popular and jovial, Joe was a regular attraction on the Indian polo circuit. At fifty, he finally married his childhood chum Vidya, daughter of Maharani Gayatri Devi's Cooch Behar relations.

Soft-spoken Pat was sent to learn business management from one of India's top industrialists, the Jaipur-born G.D. Birla. He went on to become influential in the hotel and travel industries in India, which now involve so many royal families.

Even the youngest son, Jagat, had to prepare for a career while his father lived. Jagat went through a long-haired hippy phase and a brief marriage to a bright Thai princess, Priya.

The Jaipur family has been active in politics. Maharani Gayatri Devi was elected to the Lok Sabha (the lower house of India's bicameral legislature) as a representative of the Swatantra Party (after refusing to join the ruling Congress party) by an incredible margin of 175,000 votes. Man Singh was a member of the Rajya Sabha (the upper house of India's bicameral legislature). Pat and Joe have also been elected to the Lok Sabha and the Rajasthan State Assembly.

With Nehru's death, a new spirit of accommodation towards the princes was seen. The new Prime Minister, Lal Bahadur Shastri, made Yuvraj Lalit Sen of Suket his parliamentary secretary; Maharaja Karan Singh of Jammu and Kashmir, the Gaekwad of Baroda, the Mysore Maharaja and the present Rajmatas of Gwalior and Patiala were among his advisors. Man Singh was appointed ambassador to Spain.

After Shastri's death, Indira Gandhi became Prime Minister. She made it clear that the princes were an anachronism in a democratic socialist republic, and set about abolishing their powers, privileges and privy purses. Notices were sent to the princes informing them about their derecognition. The princes appealed to the Supreme Court and won the case. But immediately after the Bangladesh war in 1971, the Constitution was amended, enabling the derecognition of the princes, and the abolition of their titles, privileges and privy purses by an Act of Parliament.

There were further shocks in store for the Jaipur royal family. Jai Garh Fort, the legendary hiding place of the treasures amassed by Kachwaha rulers, and Moti Doongri, where Gayatri Devi lived, were raided by Income Tax authorities. All the jewellery, gold and silver were, however, found to be legitimate. But twenty-odd pounds were found, which amounted to a violation of the Foreign Exchange Regulation Act. Immediately after the declaration of Emergency in 1975, Gayatri Devi was arrested for this minor FERA violation. Her stepson, Colonel Bhawani Singh, a decorated war hero, who tried to reason with the officials, was also arrested.

Man Singh was spared this ignominy. He died on May 24, 1970, while holidaying in England. His body was flown back to Jaipur, where the entire state bade him farewell. Nearly half-a-million people watched the funeral cortege, and over twenty million people followed it to Galta, where his heir, Bubbles, performed his last rites according to ancient Hindu tradition, assisted by his three half-brothers, Joe, Pat and Jagat. For the Jaipur house it was the end of an era.

chapter **6**

Monumental Achievements

To the eye, Jaipur offers a landscape of opulence that tells of a magnificent and bygone but always well-built era. It was Sawai Jai Singh who kick-started construction by building the city, his palace and five observatories in a span of 11 years

MAHARAJA BAWANI SINGH SITS FOR THE *SHASTRA POOJA*, THE WORSHIP OF ARMS, PERFORMED DURING DUSSEHRA

Facing page: THE BIRTHDAY CELEBRATION OF BHAWANI SINGH, WHO NOW LIVES IN CITY PALACE

Preceding pages 56-57: THE FORT OF NAHARGARH FURNISHES A VIEW OF THE CITY'S URBAN SPRAWL

THE VIEW OF AMBER, JAIGARH, NAHARGARH, AND THE fortified clifftop on which they stand, makes a powerful impact no matter how often one experiences it.

Amber's proximity to the ancient kingdom of Bairath (in present-day Alwar), of which mention is made in the *Mahabharata* (an Indian epic), lends credibility to the belief that it was originally founded by King Ambarish, a contemporary of Lord Krishna. Centuries later, a Mina fortress dominated the pass which straddled the highway connecting Delhi, Mewar, Marwar, Malwa, Gujarat and the Deccan. The Kachwahas simply occupied and enlarged this stronghold, turning Amber into their capital, and Jaigarh into their garrison. From their ramparts one can see two valleys, full of rustling date palms and yellow-flowered *kikar* (a thorny bush), the flat plain on which Jaipur stands, and the rocky ravines which merge into Ajmer's higher hills. In the monsoon, three streams water this region, but at other times life survives on the offerings of lakes and wells. Houses, temples, mosques and gardens are reflected in the moat and lakes below. Between them move painted elephants for tourist hire, colourfully-clad women, boisterous children, and turbanned men riding camels, bullock carts, cars and cycles.

A steep stone-paved rampart leads to Amber. Like every Rajput fort, it had been built gradually—numerous kings and queens adding palaces, gardens, pavilions and temples to the original fort, which Man Singh had enlarged and embellished over half a century.

Warriors once guarded Amber's main gateway, Vijay Pol (victory gate), and kept watch over the surrounding countryside from its towers. Here the *Naubat Khana* (music gallery) sounded both welcome and warning, with different drumbeats.

Steps from a nearby double-arched doorway lead to Shila Devi's shrine. The image of the universal mother in her war goddess aspect that resides here was brought to Amber from Bengal by Raja Man Singh in 1604. Green marble pillars carved in the shape of banana trees, and solid silver doors embossed with images of Hindu gods

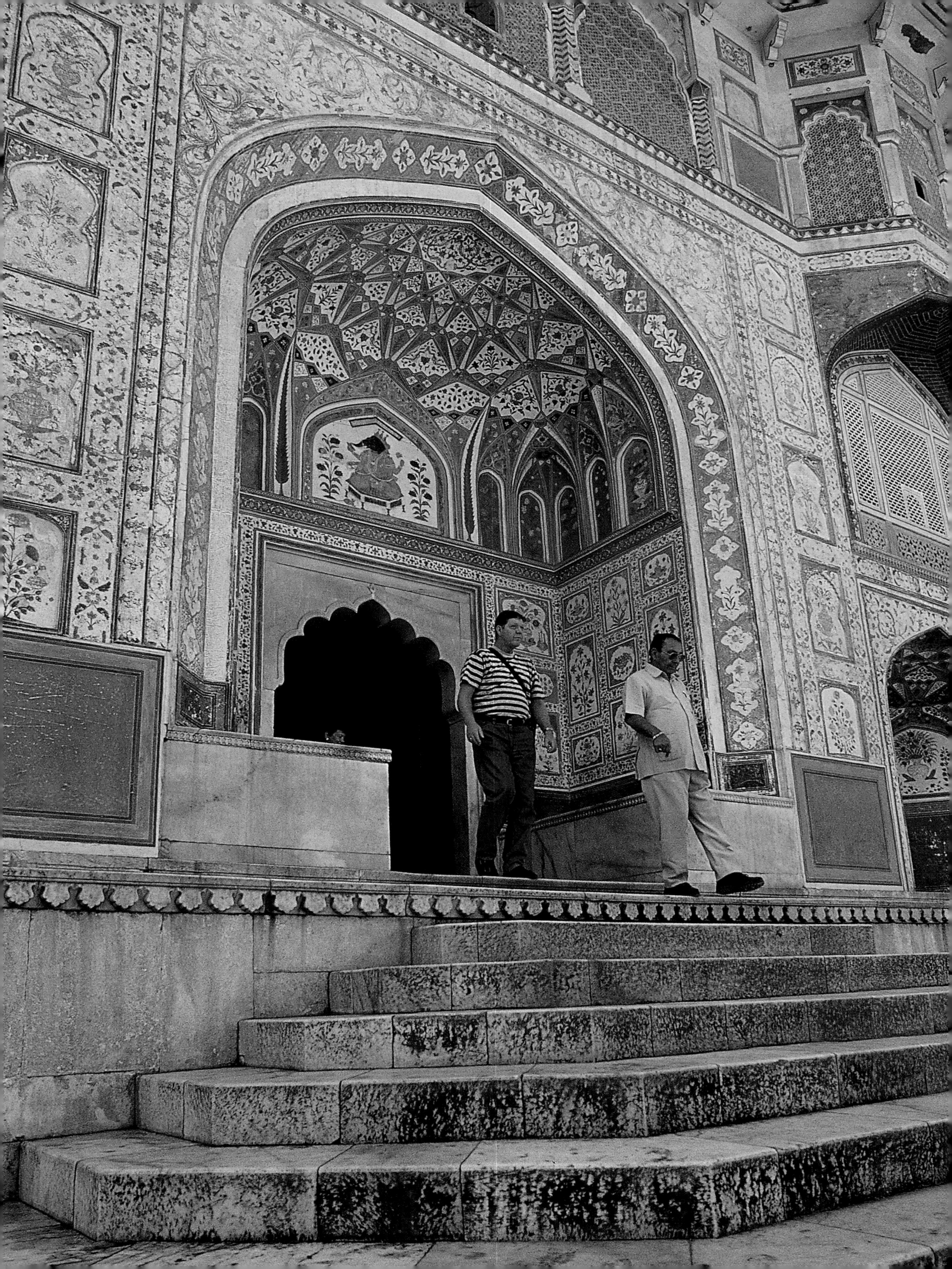

BELOW THE COLONNADED ARCHES OF *SATTAIS KATCHERI* (THE HALL OF 27 COURTS) IN AMBER FORT, *MUNIMS* OR ACCOUNTANTS ONCE SAT TO KEEP THE REVENUE RECORDS
Facing page: GANESH POL OR ELEPHANT GATE, SO CALLED BECAUSE OF THE GANESH IMAGE PAINTED ABOVE THE DOORWAY

and goddesses, adorn this temple which is still the private property of the former rulers of Jaipur. Amber, Jaigarh and Nahargarh were handed over to Rajasthan's archaeology department to ensure their proper maintenance.

The gorgeous three-storeyed Ganesh Pol (Ganesh gate) was built by Jai Singh I. Here, a lifesize Ganesh—the elephant-faced Hindu god of wisdom and good fortune—is surrounded by colourful mosaic panels, recessed painted arches, *mirhabs* (arches), and a profusion of latticed windows. From three airy *jharokhas* (balconies), royal ladies watched the arrival and departure of Amber's kings, and their turbanned and bejewelled kinsmen riding richly caparisoned elephants and horses, followed by colourful retinues, and warriors in clinking chain mail carrying shields, swords and spears. This courtyard still seems to resound with martial music from booming *naggaras* (kettle drums), clashing cymbals, high-pitched oboes and frenzied *ranbheris* (war trumpets).

Through Ganesh Pol one steps into a formal Mughal garden. Here, the highly Persianised Mirza Raja Jai Singh built his pleasure pavilion, Sukh Niwas. Fountains and water channels cooled this hall. The Jai Mandir apartment has superb floral and cypress-tree murals on plaster walls and ceilings, polished to rival marble. Once there were precious stones in Amber's *pietra dura* decorations. Now only the gold paint and mirror work remain. The pillared Diwan-i-aam, where public durbars were held, and justice dispensed, has also suffered the ravages of time.

The view from the Jai Mandir's incredible floor-to-ceiling carved alabaster window arches are still superb. But royal Jaipur's forest cover is long gone. Formal entertainments, and specially dances, were held in the mirror-encrusted Sheesh Mahal, where the flame from a single candle was reflected a thousand times. The Amber *zenana* is small and dingy compared to the *zenana* palaces of Jodhpur, Bundi or Bikaner. Its charming terraced garden was created by a Kashmiri princess married to Jai Singh I. Kesar Bai pined for the fragrant saffron fields of her Himalayan homeland, and actually succeeded in growing it with cartloads of soil brought from Kashmir by her doting husband.

The Jaigarh Fort behind Amber was the true Kachwaha stronghold to which the Kachwahas retreated when faced with external attack or strife within. A defensive fortress complex consisting of ramparts, watchtowers, gateways, chambers, temples and large tanks, Jaigarh was the traditional cache for the fabulous Kachwaha treasures acquired over centuries by Jaipur's victorious armies. The Mina tribe from whom Amber was originally wrested by Dhola Rai became its traditional keepers. How each Kachwaha king was taken blindfolded into the secret vaults through secret passages known only to the Mina headman and his son is part of folklore. Minas have perished under torture without revealing Jaigarh's secrets, for they firmly believed that this ancestral wealth was only

to be used for protecting the kingdom, and not for the king's pleasure. Maharaja Man Singh II had a jewelled gold eagle which he swore came from this secret hoard. His heir Bubbles smiles and shrugs away all inquisitive queries.

Many historians believe that Jaigarh's true treasure was its cannon foundry, which gave the Kachwahas an edge over their rivals. The enormous Jaivan cannon which still stands guard over Jaipur is a masterpiece. Said to be Asia's largest cannon, it is a magnificent example of the ancient Indian arts of iron, steel and bronze casting. A symbol of Kachwaha power, this three-hundred-year-old cannon is kept shining, and is blessed every year when the Maharaja performs the Dussehra Shastra Puja (weapon worship).

Six kilometres from Jaigarh's stark stronghold stands a very different royal home. Nahargarh's luxurious pavilions, gardens and galleries provided Jaipur's kings and queens with a summer retreat. Today tour groups, children, goats, monkeys and stray ponies scramble up and down this steep hilltop park.

Originally constructed by Jai Singh II, Nahargarh was improved and enlarged by his youngest son and ultimate successor, Madho Singh. His reign was turbulent, with Marathas, Mughals, Jats, Pathans, and his own Rajput kinsmen, continually attacking Jaipur. Nahargarh was more secure than the City Palace, so Madho Singh fortified the open spaces around this pleasure park, and made a steep rampart, leading down the hill, with secret tunnels connecting it with the City Palace.

In 1860, Ram Singh II commissioned nine identical apartments with wall frescoes, carved door panels with decorative handles, metal ceiling fan rings with lacwork designs, fireplaces and Belgian glass mirrors for his nine queens. From the airy terraces and jutting balconies one gets an excellent view of the lakes, hills, old bastions, temples, and the cluster of houses that make up Jaipur and Amber.

Several ancient Jain and Hindu shrines, including the Jagat Shiromani temple built by Raja Bhar Mal, are scattered through this old town.

The royal *chattris* at Galta evoke memories of bygone maharajas. Kachwaha kings often had to take recourse to adoptions outside the immediate family for heirs, and the identity of the adopted heir was often disclosed only after the reigning king's death. This lent a certain degree of uncertainty to the performance of his last rites and the building of a cenotaph in his name. Kachwaha kings thus usually designed and built their own funereal monuments. Man

SHEESH MAHAL AT AMBER HAS AN INTERIOR THAT RADIATES WITH THOUSANDS OF TINY MIRRORS
Facing page: THE JAIVANA, BELIEVED TO BE THE LARGEST CANON IN THE WORLD, HAS NEVER BEEN FIRED
Preceding pages 62-63: JAIPUR STRAGGLES UP TO THE OLD NAHARGARH WALL IN THIS PHOTOGRAPH SHOT FROM THE JAIGARH-NAHARGARH ROAD

Singh II, notwithstanding four sons by three wives, commissioned a stately marble monument which was completed—and paid for—during his lifetime. The queens and princesses were cremated at a separate spot overlooked by Galta's Sun Temple.

Among Amber's royal gardens, two have been restored and opened to the public. The Dilaram garden has an interesting archaeological museum where decorated pre-Harappan pottery, ancient Indo-Aryan sculpture, Ashokan pillars, Gandhara coins, Jain statues, medieval terracotta toys and Persian-style glazed tiles are displayed.

The square Jal Mahal Palace, surrounded by the Man Sagar Lake, has airy domes, pavilions and terraces around an old fruit orchard. From here the Maharaja and his guests often shot migrating geese, grouse and duck in winter.

When Jai Singh II wed the Mewar princess Chandra Kanwar, the marriage contract stipulated that her wishes be honoured. She desired a private garden retreat, so Jai Singh built the Sisodia Rani Ka Bagh, beyond Ghat Lake, where water was available. The site testifies to her superb confidence and genuine courage—this pleasure park, created exclusively for women, was miles away from Jaipur's well-guarded City Palace, and fortified Amber, in the days when Jaipur was continually under siege.

The palace walls are covered on the inside and outside with

frescoes of hunting scenes, polo players, dancing girls and strolling lovers, in the Shekhawati style. From the domed rooftop and the chambers one can look down on perfectly spaced fountains, pools, pavilions, lawns, flower beds, flowering shrubs and shady fruit trees. Even more charming is the view of wooded valleys and craggy hills crowned with crumbling temples and browsing deer. Peacocks, parrots, squirrels, goats, cows and red-faced langurs inhabit the courtyards that are surrounded by shrines. The black marble Vishnu statue, the eleven *shivlingas,* and an image of Parvati (Shiva's consort) were installed by Jai Singh's Sisodia queen after she became a widow.

The Galta Sun Temple on a nearby hillock has a perennial spring which flows from the mouth of a stone cow and fills seven tanks. It is reputed to have magical curative powers.

Sawai Jai Singh built Jaipur city, his own palace and five observatories between 1724 and 1735 with the help of a Bengali architect called Vidyadhar. The walled city was meticulously planned, and each community or guild was given its own quarters—the jewellers had Johri Bazaar; the dyers Neelgaro ka Mohalla; and the sculptors Shilagaro ka Rasta. In order to defend his kingdom better, the shrewd Maharaja settled the feudatory warlords of Chomu and Samode near the Dhroov Gate, the Rajas of Sikar and Khetri at Chand Pol, the Uniara and Diggi *thakurs* (feudal lords) at Ajmeri Gate, and the Jhalai and Isarda *thakurs* at Suraj Pol. All administrative offices were located at Brahma Pol—Jai Singh evidently believed in the wisdom of keeping his nobility, intelligentsia, and the craftsmen and labourers, separate from each other.

The City Palace is actually a city within a city: here thousands were once employed to serve the ruling Kachwahas. Palaces, temples, gardens, offices,

residential quarters, workshops, stables and workhouses were all laid out according to Jai Singh's master plan.

Huge pink Bengal-arch gateways covered with white floral motifs lead to the City Palace. Tripolia is the royal ceremonial gate. Until 1970, the *Naubat Khana* over the Dhundhubi Pol resounded with music every time the Maharaja entered or left the City Palace. All the gatehouses have soldiers' quarters. Six gates have to be passed before one reaches the Diwan-i-aam.

Lamp posts of red sandstone add colour to the white limestone-and-shellac walls of most City Palace buildings. Spacious courtyards surround each palace, and turbanned retainers guide the flow of paying sightseers.

All investiture ceremonies up to that of Bhawani Singh in 1970 have been held in Jai Singh's Diwan-i-khas (private durbar hall), popularly called the Sarbatta. The Sarbatta has been many things to many kings: here Pratab Singh met scholars, poets and philosophers; Ram Singh II held special banquets; and Madho Singh entertained viceroys and visiting royalty. After Independence, Man Singh and Gayatri Devi entertained visiting dignitaries in this impressive hall.

The pyramidal Chandra Mahal is the City Palace's most remarkable building. Vidyadhar, Jai Singh's chief architect, designed the original seven-storeyed palace. Subsequent rulers made their own additions to the original structure. In 1976, Bhawani Singh

moved into the City Palace with his wife and daughter to prevent its acquisition by the government as a historical monument. They live upstairs in Chandra Mahal, host dinners for tourist groups, and allow film units to use the palace for authentic location shoots.

The exquisite doorways that date back to Jai Singh II's days are the main attractions of the Chandra Mahal courtyard. The Peacock Gate is ornamented with lifesize plaster peacocks. The undulating arches of the Seashell Gate shimmer sea-green and gold around silver-inlaid doors. The surrounding colonnades, marble floors, iron pillars, and portraits of his ancestors by the German painter A.H. Muller, are Man Singh II's contribution. He also set up the City Palace Museum which draws huge crowds.

Sawai Jai Singh built the second storey, Sukh Niwas, for his favourite queen, Sukh Kanwar, mother of Ishwari Singh. This became her artistic grandson Pratab Singh's favourite residence. Its walls are decorated with *pietra dura* floral motifs and gold-leaf scrolls. Pratab commissioned the ground floor of the Pritam Niwas and the Riddhi-Siddhi Pol.

Inlaid mirror work being a Jaipur speciality, Sawai Jai Singh's Sheesh Mahal was famous even at the Mughal court. The other remarkable chamber is the Rang Mandir, whose walls, pillars and ceiling are encrusted with coloured glass. Shobha Niwas, Chhabi Niwas and Shri Niwas on the fourth, fifth and sixth floors are also

SISODIA RANI KA BAGH WAS BUILT AS A PRIVATE GARDEN RETREAT FOR THE MEWAR PRINCESS CHANDRA KANWAR, ACCORDING TO THE MARRIAGE CONTRACT JAI SINGH II HAD WITH HER

Facing page 66: JAL MAHAL, A PALACE SURROUNDED BY WATER WAS A FORMER HUNTING LODGE, AND IS TODAY THE MOST ROMANTICALLY EXQUISITE RETREAT

TREASURES OF THE CITY PALACE

1

Built by Sawai Jai Singh, the City Palace is fit for gods. It boasts of the world's finest collection of miniature paintings and includes the Sheesh Mahal, the Sukh Niwas and the colour-glass wonder, Rang Mandir.

2

3

5

4

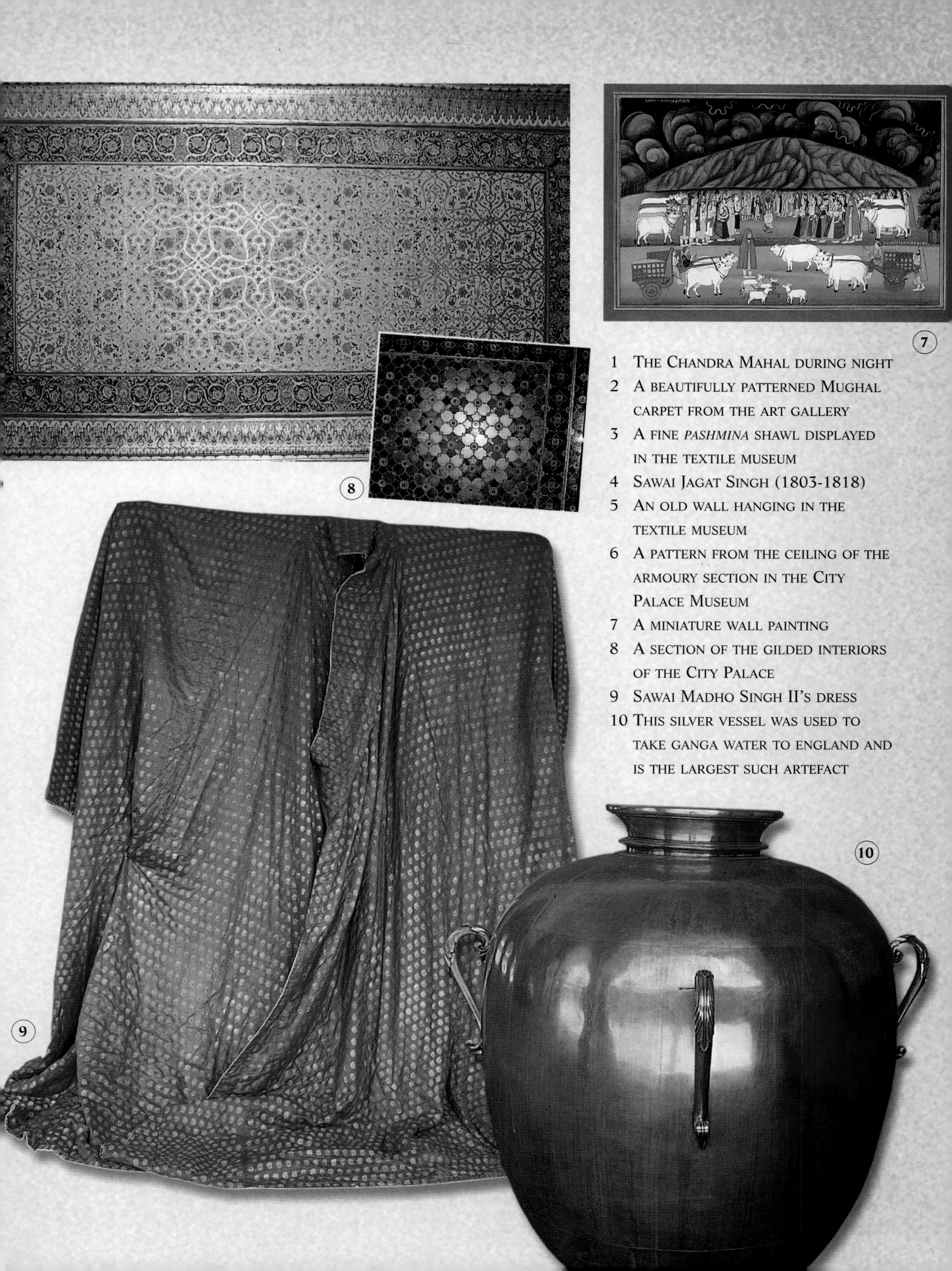

1 The Chandra Mahal during night
2 A beautifully patterned Mughal carpet from the art gallery
3 A fine *pashmina* shawl displayed in the textile museum
4 Sawai Jagat Singh (1803-1818)
5 An old wall hanging in the textile museum
6 A pattern from the ceiling of the armoury section in the City Palace Museum
7 A miniature wall painting
8 A section of the gilded interiors of the City Palace
9 Sawai Madho Singh II's dress
10 This silver vessel was used to take Ganga water to England and is the largest such artefact

The City Palace complex with Chandra Mahal in the background

Facing page 71: The Diwan-e-Khas (hall for private audience) in the City Palace

Following pages 72-73: The Sobha Niwas can well be seen as a centrepiece of glitz and glitter. It was in effect a highly ornate sitting room for the Maharajas and could not be beaten for sheer wealth of ornamentation

richly ornamented. Royal couples traditionally performed *puja* (ritual worship) to Laxmi, Goddess of wealth, on the occasion of Diwali (the festival of lights) in the Shobha Niwas.

Maharaja Ram Singh II used the Chandra Mahal's spacious rooftop terraces to fly his special paper kites, ornamented with silver bells, during the Akha Teej festival, vying with all comers for airspace. He seldom had any success in getting back any of the kites he lost in duels, for they were prized souvenirs for his subjects.

Ram Singh II had gifted an excellent property to Kesar Badaran, the chief maid of his two Rewa queens. This garden, known as Badaran-ka-bagh, became Rambagh Palace when her property passed back to the king in accordance with the law of escheat, which the Jaipur rulers had borrowed from the Mughals. Maharaja Ram Singh used it as a shooting lodge, extending it to accommodate the Prince of Wales in 1877. Madho Singh II used it as a guest house for visiting viceroys and kings. It became a royal home when the British Resident moved Man Singh II there from the City Palace.

Man Singh further extended the palace to accommodate his growing polygamous family, successfully preserving its traditional architecture. Even the most blase globe trotter can't help being charmed by its classic Rajput kiosks, Bengal-arch pavilions, cool verandahs and courtyards framed by scalloped arches and marble pillars, reflecting pools, stately terraces surrounded by unbelievably green gardens inhabited by peacocks, parrots, pigeons and dozens of other Indian birds.

The very English herbaceous borders introduced by Madho

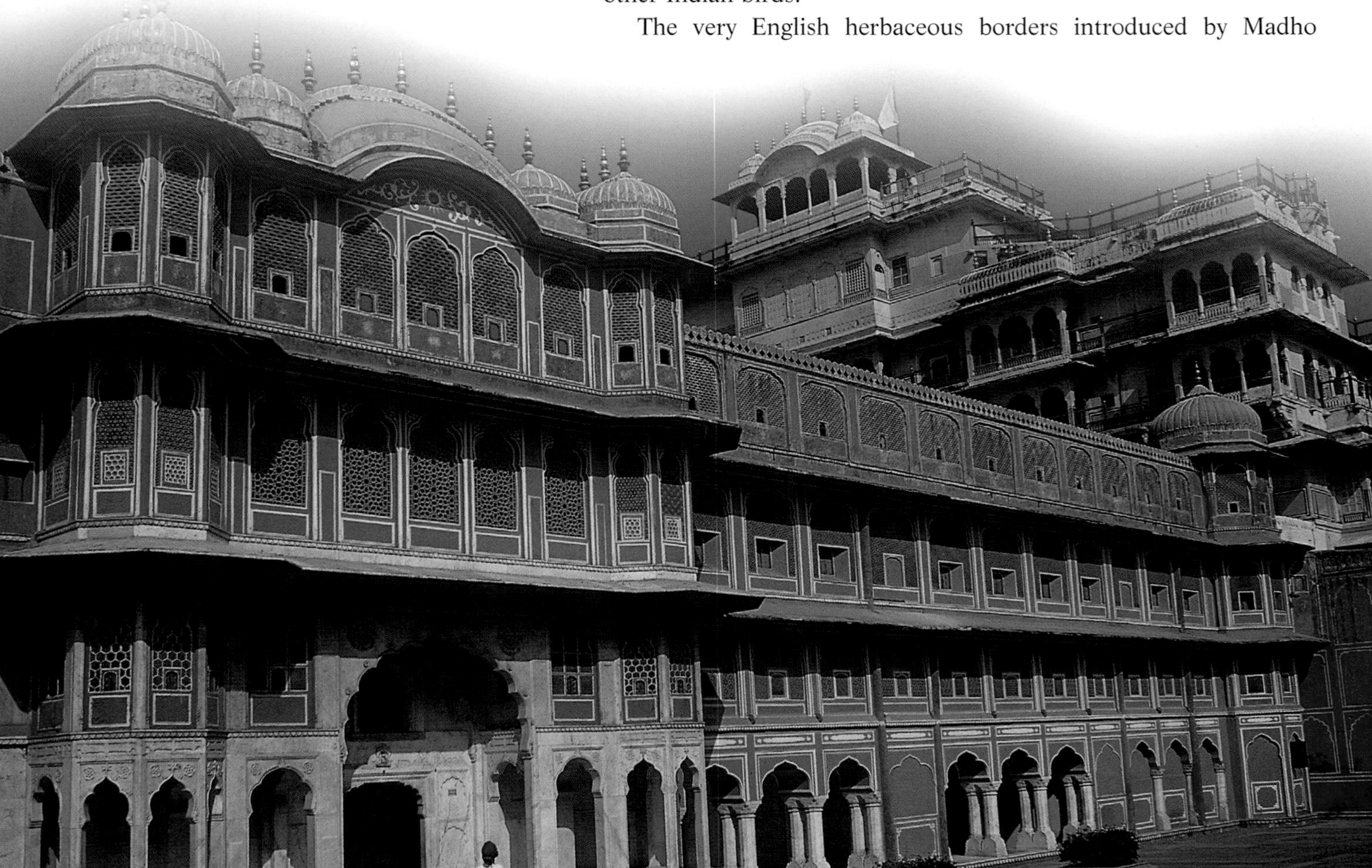

Singh II after his 1902 England visit still bloom with lupins, hollyhocks, larkspurs, poppies, petunias, snapdragons, cornflowers, daisies, phlox and stock. There are still tranquil views of hilltop castles. Except for the damaged Lalique fountains and the bustle of hotel guests one could well be in a magic realm.

The beauty and opulence of a royal era survive even after this palace has become one of the busiest hotels in India. The Polo Bar, with its colourful lamps, the triple horse-head copper wall plate, polo prints and cane furniture is still the starting point for great parties. The lovely Chinese room, the Princess Suite with its sunken marble mosaic fountain, the spacious Maharaja Suite with its black marble bathtub are still royal treats.

Lalique objets d'art were a weakness with Man Singh. He also collected a great deal of common European bric-a-brac and furniture, and the obligatory crystal, English bone china, Belgian cut-glass, marble statues and oil paintings. The gaudy damasks, velvets and shiny jacquards at Rambagh reveal his Isarda origins.

It was Gayatri Devi, with her flair for fashion and exquisite aesthetic sensibility, who brought a touch of class to Jaipur's royal homes. Her personal collection of jade, rose quartz, smoky topaz, jewelled daggers, enamelled Jaipur gold and silver animals, birds and boxes are as discriminatingly selected as the Victoria and Albert Museum's India Collection. The best Mughal and Rajasthani miniatures, portraits, and Persian and Afghan carpets have found their way into Moti Doongri, Rambagh and Raj Mahal.

Rambagh was created for entertaining a very exclusive international clique. The polo ground, riding tracks, indoor swimming pool, tennis and squash courts, and extensive grounds presented ample opportunities for healthy sports. In the evenings, music and dancing enlivened dinner parties. Traditional Rajasthani entertainment was laid on for special guests, and on special occasions.

Raj Mahal is a rambling but comfortable mansion that was owned by Ram Singh II's mother, Maharani Chandrawatiji. She permitted the British to use it as their Residency when Colonel Ludlow became her son's guardian. In 1976, when Bubbles moved back into the City Palace, Raj Mahal too was converted into a hotel. Huge royal portraits, hunting trophies, ornamental swords and shields, bronzes, carved rosewood and teak furniture, and gilt-panelled doors exude an old-world charm that is enhanced by its secluded position on Jaipur's Sardar Patel Marg.

Sawai Jai Singh's fascinating outdoor observatory attracts serious scholars and playful children alike. To pursue his hobby, astronomy, Jai Singh wanted perfectly stable astronomical instruments. While experimenting, he found that metal instruments gave incorrect

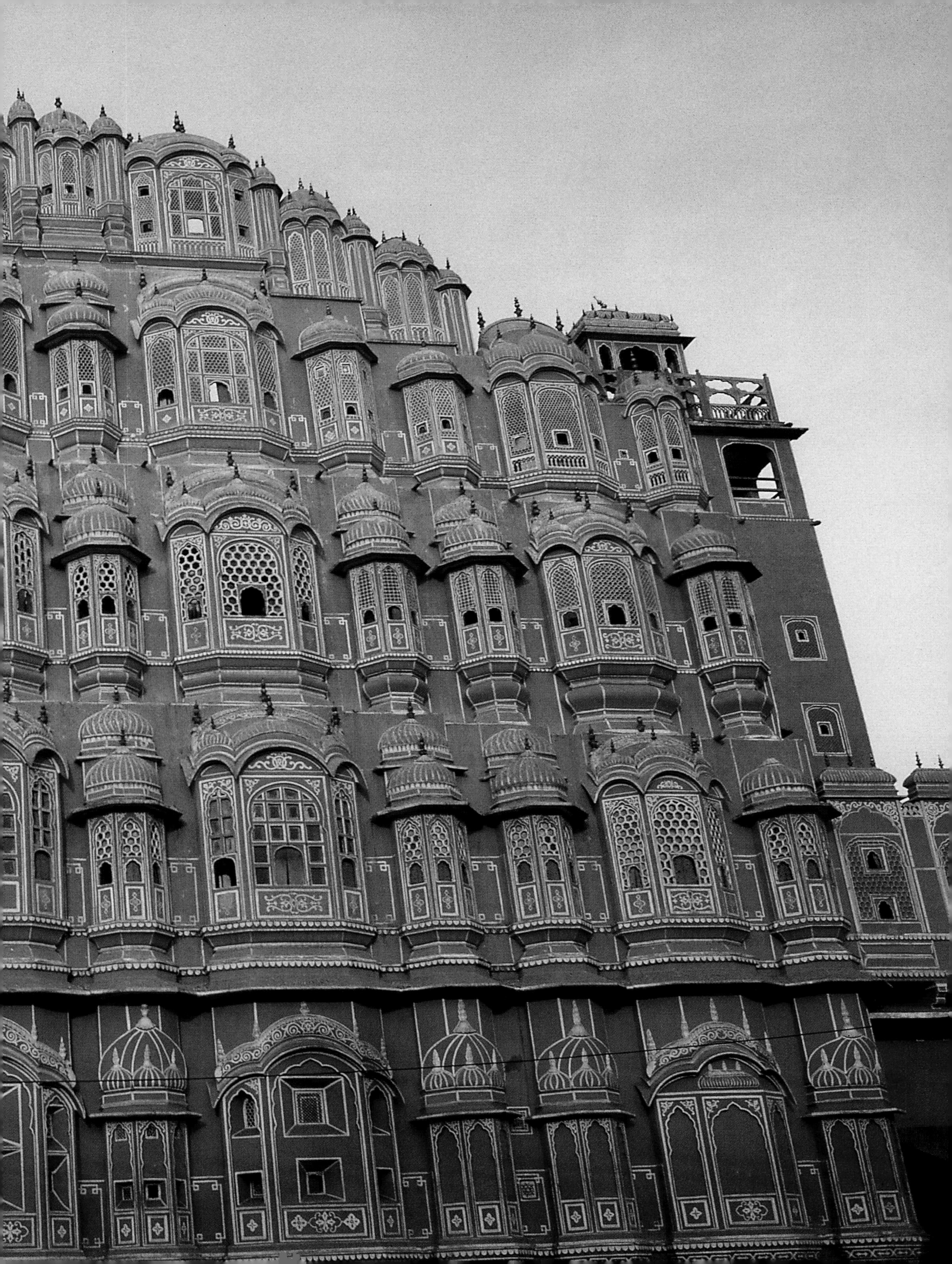

THE ARMOURY SECTION OF THE CITY PALACE MUSEUM DISPLAYS THE CRUDER WEAPONS OF AN AGE THAT HAD NOT YET SEEN TECHNOLOGY MAKE ITS ARSENAL LETHAL BUT HAD SUFFERED SUFFICIENT BLOODSHED

Pages 76-77 (bottom): THE DECISION TO CONVERT RAMBAGH PALACE INTO A HOTEL WAS TAKEN BY A FORESIGHTED MAN SINGH II

Facing page top: THE RELAXED AMBIENCE OF THE PLUSH POLO BAR AT RAMBAGH PALACE

Preceding pages 74-75: HAWA MAHAL, BUILT BY PRATAB SINGH, IS A FIVE-STOREYED PINK STUCCO FACADE WITH *JHAROKHA* WINDOWS ONCE USED BY QUEENS TO WATCH THE OUTSIDE WORLD

measurements and readings. For the sake of greater accuracy, he caused stone and mortar observatories to be constructed at five places—Jaipur, Delhi, Agra, Ujjain and Benaras. Familiar with Indian, Arabic and European star tables, he designed the Samrat, Ram and Jai Prakash Yantras, which scholars can still use to verify star positions. His Samrat Yantra, centred on the North Star, is an amazing time-keeper. After 250 years, it has lost none of its accuracy.

Ishwari Singh built the seven-storey Isar Lat (Isar's tower) in 1749 to commemorate Jaipur's victory over the combined forces of seven Maratha, Mughal and Rajput generals. The open galleries of this octagonal tower, enclosed by carved stone balustrades, provide a panoramic view of the cityscape below. The tower adjoins

Chaugan, Jaipur's public entertainment ground, where polo, elephant fights and other sports were held between 1724 and 1921. The stables and *Peel Khana* (elephant stalls) being adjacent, it was easy to transport the animals. Teej and Gangaur (important Rajasthani Hindu festivals) processions also gathered here after going through the city. Three other octagonal towers overlooked the Chaugan. From these the ruler and his family, chiefs and ministers watched fairs, wrestling matches and other displays. The first tower is called Chini Burj, because it is decorated with Chinese willow-pattern tiles. The British Resident and other Europeans sat here. The Moti Burj was reserved for the Maharaja, and the Chattar Burj for his principal courtiers. The royal ladies watched from an enclosed verandah they entered through passages from the *zenani dyodhi* and Chandra Mahal.

Pratab Singh built the Hawa Mahal as a vantage point from which his queens and female relations could watch the outside world and amuse themselves during his long absences from home. A five-storeyed pink stucco facade, painted with white flowering vines and geometric trees, the Hawa Mahal is an inseparable part of the memories of royal Jaipur. The pierced stucco *jharokha* windows are as delicate and fragile as the women they once screened from the public gaze. The vibrancy of Tripolia Bazaar, even more crowded and colourful today with the intermingling of the old and the new, is obvious to every visitor.

Entering Hawa Mahal from the main west-facing gate, one finds a large paved courtyard surrounded by verandahs and rooms, where royal ladies rested while watching lengthy processions and religious festivals. Another courtyard has a square marble pool where Holi was celebrated with great gusto by these ladies. The doorways to both these courtyards are flanked by statues of Hindu deities.

Pratab Singh also constructed a large pool behind Govind Devji's temple, and the quaint Sawan-Bhadon Pavilion, where unwary guests were often surprised by sudden showers from concealed fountains. Ram Singh II's marble-pillared and *pietra dura*-decorated billiard room near Sawan-Bhadon was converted into a banquet hall by Sawai Man Singh in 1933.

The Jai Niwas Mahal Garden behind Chandra Mahal was laid out by Sawai Jai Singh in the traditional Mughal style, with traditional lawns, ornamental trees, flower beds, fountains, reflecting pools, paved walks and pavilions. He lived in the small Badal Mahal before Chandra Mahal was ready. The beauty of Jai Niwas Garden has now been ruined by the houses that crowd around the Talkatora Lake. The fruit orchard adjoining the garden has been opened to the public by the present Maharaja.

Mubarak Mahal, now the curator's office and the textile museum, was built in 1896 by Maharaja Madho Singh as a guest house. This airy double-storeyed palace with its slender pillars, lattice-work windows, projecting balconies, carved balustrades and painted windows, reflects the architectural styles of Kathmandu and Kangra. Nearby stands the Clock Tower, beyond which Jai Singh's observatory can be seen from Mubarak Mahal's balconies.

From Mubarak Mahal, the Maharaja's guests reached the Sarbatta through Shri Dyodhi, a richly ornamented gateway with Bengal-arch pavilions, marble fretwork windows and pillared arches. The two marble elephants standing guard were installed on the first birthday of the present Maharaja by his proud father.

In Rajput states, rulers were expected to honour the gods and perform the right rituals at the right time of the year to ensure public prosperity. To be known as a *dharma atman* (pious soul) was the highest form of acclaim for anyone. The Kachwaha rulers, therefore, built many impressive temples in Amber and Jaipur.

The hilltop Galta Math is an ancient Hindu monastery where disciples studied Sanskrit, Vedic scriptures, yoga, meditation, philosophy, ethics, logic, ayurvedic medicine and astrology under renowned scholars. This holy place was given an annual grant by the Jaipur rulers, plus generous gifts by their queens and kinsmen.

Like the Mewar kings who ruled as Eklingji's *dewans*, the Jaipur rulers called themselves Gobind Devji's *dewans*. The lovely Gobind Dev Temple stands near the Suraj Mahal Baradari in the Jai Niwas Garden between the Chandra and Badal Mahals. When Sawai Jai Singh started developing and building Jaipur, he lived in this Baradari until he heard in a dream: 'This place belongs to God. Leave it.'

The very next day, Jai Singh shifted to Badal Mahal and laid the foundations of Gobind Devji's temple in the Bara-dari.. A double row of carved marble pillars and a high, girderless, cantilevered roof give this shrine an illusion of space. Legend has it that a king from the *Mahabharata* era, Vajra Nabh of Bairath, first built a temple on this spot for Lord Krishna, also called Gobind. But the king's mother felt that the statue installed in the temple was not a true likeness of Krishna. A second statue was also rejected before the dowager queen expressed her satisfaction at the third attempt. The original icon has been lost. The present one was presented to Raja Man Singh by the great Bhakti saint, Chaitanya Mahaprabhu. The accompanying statue of Radha was a gift from Raja Rudra Pratap of Orissa. In 1590, when Raja Man Singh installed these beautiful pink sandstone statues, Akbar and his wife Jodhabai offered prayers here. A *jagir* took care of the temple's upkeep in the olden days. After the abolition of the princely states, the Jaipur Maharaja settled Rs. 32,000 annually on this temple for its maintenance.

The original Kachwaha family deity was Sitaramji. Amber's rulers built a temple to this deity in 1226 in the original fort, which is now part of Jaigarh. This serene Ram-Hari-Vishnu temple has been beautified by later rulers. The original silver statues were given to Raja Prithviraj and his bride Bala Bai by Sant Krishna Das Padihar, then Abbot of Galta. It was only during the fifteenth and sixteenth centuries, when the Bhakti movement inspired a wave of Vaishnavism, that the Kachwahas adopted Krishna as their personal deity. However, the Sitaramji icons retained a special place. They were always carried by the vanguard by Jaipur armies in times of war.

The lovely royal temple that few know about is Lakshman Dwara. It houses *asthadhatu* (an eight-metal alloy) images of Tirupati (Lord of the three worlds) and his consort Shri Devi, brought from ancient Vijaynagar in South India.

The impressive Brij Nandan Temple was made by Sawai Pratab Singh, a Krishna worshipper. It is built like an eighteenth-century *haveli* (mansion), with an iron-studded gate. Contemporary records show that the Radha statue was installed only after a magnificent wedding ceremony at the Johri Bazaar Haveli of Pratab Singh's *dewan,* Daulat Ram Haldia. Even today, the Haldia family maintain a fraternal relationship with this Radha Rani, sending traditional gifts on religious functions like Janamasthami (Krishna's birthday), Diwali and Teej.

Ram Singh II worshipped Shiva, and built the Raj Rajeshwar temple between the *zenani* and *shriji dyodhis.* It is the only royal temple which is not open to the public. Excellent wall paintings of Shiva, Parvati, Ganesha, Rama, Sita, and episodes from the *Shiva Purana* embellish the *shivayala* (abode of Shiva) with its polished stone *lingam* (phallus). A huge brass Nandi (Shiva's bull) sits facing this in the corridor outside.

Madho Singh II built the twin temples of Gopalji and Gangaji. Steps connect these temples which face each other. They are surrounded by pillars, carved balconies and green lawns. Honouring old Hindu traditions, he insisted on drinking only Ganga water brought to Jaipur all the way from Hardwar, where the water enters the plains from the snow-covered Himalaya. When the British government launched a scheme to build dams and regulators over the Ganga near the Har Ki Pauri, a spot sacred to Hindus, Madho Singh teamed up with Madan Mohan Malaviya, a nationalist leader and a protagonist of the Hindu Mahasabha, to organise a religious-cum-environmental conference at Hardwar, and successfully pressured the British into modifying these projects.

SAWAI JAI SINGH'S OBSERVATORY AT JAIPUR IS ONE OF THE FIVE HE BUILT USING STONE AND MORTAR, NOT METALS, FOR GREATER ACCURACY

Following page 80: A 16TH-CENTURY, LATTICED STAINED GLASS WINDOW IN AMBER FORT IS TYPICAL OF THE MANY THAT GIVE FINE SHADES TO JAIPUR'S ARCHITECTURAL STYLE

Sanganer's magnificent Jain temples, and the numerous mosques and *mazars* (tombs of saints) spread all over their kingdom, bear testimony to the Jaipur rulers' respect for all religions. Since the days of Mirza Raja Jai Singh, a gold and silver *tazia* (banner) presented by him leads the Muharram (the ten-day period of Muslim mourning) procession in this state every year. Jaipur was also the only Rajput state, apart from Jodhpur, which allowed Catholics to build churches and open schools there.

chapter 7

The Art of Patronage

The kings were themselves artists and, when not, very able collectors of texts, paintings, jewellery, furniture... Jaipur became the hub for artists after the 1857 Mutiny when many of them who fled Delhi found refuge in the city

THE KACHWAHAS OF RAJPUTANA WERE LIBERAL PATRONS of the arts, crafts and learning, and many of them were as much at home with scholars and artists as they were in the world of statesmanship and the battlefield, even if their legacies were sometimes squandered.

Sawai Man Singh created an art gallery where rotating exhibitions of ancestral art treasures were held, until a family feud over the trust he had created, following his death, put a stop to it.

Mubarak Mahal still houses a superb collection of historic armour. This armoury contains the personal arms of warrior kings like Raja Man Singh, Ram Singh, the two Jai Singhs, Ishwari Singh, Madho Singh and Pratab Singh. There are swords from Persia, Damascus, Europe and India, with silver handles, hilts inlaid with gems, inscribed blades, and scabbards made of silk, velvet or beaten gold. These seem more like works of art than weapons of destruction. Muskets, muzzle-loaders, pistols, bows and arrows, ornamented quivers, inlaid wood, mother-of-pearl and ivory adorn the walls. Battle axes, ingenious sword-sticks, and steel *bagh nakh* (tiger claws) contribute to the martial ambience. Effete manicure sets, back-scratchers and betel-nut choppers, however, alleviate the menacing aura.

Another portion of Mubarak Mahal houses textiles and costumes used by Jaipur's royalty. Shahtoosh and Pashmina shawls from Kashmir, brocades from Benaras and Aurangabad, Dhaka mulmul veils and turbans, Khenkhab silks, embroidered Gujarati and Sindhi *lehengas* (long skirts), superb Rajasthani

SCIONS OF THE SHAHPURA FAMILY, A *THIKANA* OR FIEFDOM. *THIKANAS* COMMANDED LOYALTY, HAD THEIR OWN *DURBARS* AND PROVIDED HEIRS TO THE THRONE WHEN IT HAD NO NATURAL SON
Facing page: SANJAY SINGH, HEAD OF THE BISSAU *THIKANA*, WITH HIS SON. IN THE PAST, BISSAU WAS INDEPENDENT; NOW SINGH HAS CHANGED THE FAMILY HOME INTO A GRAND HOTEL

ceremonial costumes, colourful Sanganeri and Multani prints, gold and silver *zardozi* (intricate embroidery with gold and silver threads), work veils, jewelled tassels and velvet robes fill upright cases in rooms where little sunlight penetrates to damage these royal garments.

Among the musical instruments of the former maharajas is the interesting Origami collection of Ishwari Singh. He was also responsible for launching Sanganer's handmade paper industry.

Paintings, illuminated manuscripts, antique Persian-style carpets made in Jaipur, gold and silver howdahs, palanquins and sedan chairs with gold-embroidered velvet covers for queens, are displayed in the darkened Diwan-i-khas.

The City Palace collection of Indian miniature paintings from the Mughal, Deccan, Malwa, Gujarat, Mewar, Marwar, Bundi, Kotah, Bikaner and Kishangarh schools is among the world's finest. The best Jaipur paintings belong to the reign of Pratab Singh. Pratab commissioned the Ras Leela, Rag-Ragini, Barah-Maha, Geet Govinda, Nayaka, Radha-Krishna, Shiva-Parvati, Bhagwat Purana and *Mahabharata* series. The lifesize portraits of Rana Pratap, Raja Man Singh, Sawai Pratab Singh and of Krishna lifting mount Govardhan are superb examples of Indian portraiture and narrative painting. The lavish use of gold leaf and gemstones ground into colours give them vibrancy and beauty. European influences are apparent in the paintings of Ram Singh II's time, when the Jaipur school of painting ends to give way to photographs. Ram Singh became a good photographer, and some of his photographs are displayed in this museum.

The Jaipur *Pothi Khana* is a unique institution, being a combined library, art studio and writers' workshop. It houses thousands of original manuscripts from over the Indian subcontinent, Central Asia, Persia, Turkey, Arabia and Europe. These were collected over centuries by princes who were not just soldiers and statesmen, but scholars and aesthetes who knew Sanskrit, Persian, Turkish, Arabic, Hindustani and Rajasthani, and appreciated the need to preserve historic manuscripts and patronising contemporary writers.

The library was enriched by every king, and is divided into four parts. There are eight thousand invaluable illuminated manuscripts bearing the king's *khas mohar* (personal seal). The second part consists of three thousand handwritten books. Sawai Jai Singh's collection of astronomy texts, and the discursive works of Guru Ratnakar Pundarika form the third part of this library. The fourth consists of publications acquired by various members of the royal family, and dictionaries, almanacs, maps, charts and encyclopedias.

The Kachwahas patronised many poets and writers. Several kings were themselves gifted writers. In 1617, Ram Singh I compiled *Hastak Ratnavalli*, a treatise on classical Indian dance. Pratab Singh not only patronised classical Indian dance, music and painting, but was himself a writer, known for his original *Radha-Gobind Sangeet Sagar* (Songs of Radha and Krishna). The four Vedas were translated into English and French under Pratab Singh by L.K. Antonio Luis and Henry Poliarc in 1789, and presented to

the British Museum. Sawai Jai Singh's works on astronomy and astrology are well known. Ishwari Singh wrote poetry; Ram Singh wrote and translated plays, and collected dramatic works in Sanskrit, Greek, Latin, German, French, English and Hindi. Madho Singh II commissioned Swinton Jacob, Hadley and H.L. Shower to compile a pictorial gazette on Jaipur. Orient Longman published Man Singh II's *History of the Indian State Forces*. Apart from an absorbing autobiography, Gayatri Devi has also written *Government's Gateway,* and a travelogue, with Khushwant Singh and Anees Jung.

Rulers were expected to provide entertainment for the people. No festival, royal birthday or wedding was complete without songs and dances by artistes, invariably rewarded by the Maharaja.

The *Gunijan Khana* (house of celebrated artistes), set up by Mirza Raja Jai Singh in Shah Jahan's time, became part of the Jaipur royal household. The Jaipur *gharana* (school) of *khayal* singing and Kathak (a classical Indian dance) compares favourably with those of Agra, Gwalior and Benaras.

From sunrise to sunset there was music in the City Palace. Folk and classical music and dancing were taught to queens and princesses by maestros. Man Singh's younger brother, Madho, was a renowned musician of Akbar's era. Ram Singh I, Sawai Jai Singh, Madho Singh, Pratab Singh and Ram Singh II played various instruments well enough to perform at family gatherings.

Many of the musicians, jewellers, artists and craftsmen who fled Delhi after the 1857 uprising found refuge in Jaipur. Ram Singh II employed them, gave them monthly salaries and life-*jagirs*, and encouraged his noblemen to patronise them. The widows and children of the artistes of the *Gunijan Khana* received state pensions. Gauhar Jan, one of Madho Singh II's famous court singers, became a great favourite of Man Singh, who continued giving her a generous pension till her death. After Independence, these artistes were discharged. Most either migrated to Pakistan, or left for Bombay to try their luck in the film and music industries.

Jaipur's royal household was very well organised, with thirty-six departments under separate officers. The treasury, library, picture gallery, shikar *khana* and royal kitchen in the City Palace existed to provide the Maharaja and his family with comfort and luxury.

THE LAVISH SPREAD OF DIGGI HOUSE IN JAIPUR ATTESTS TO ITS SPLENDOUR
Facing page: A DANCER SWIRLS GRACEFULLY IN THE ORNATE DURBAR HALL AT SAMODE HAVELI
Preceding pages 84-85: SAMODE HAVELI HAS FRESCOED INTERIORS AND AN AIR OF EASY OPULENCE THAT SERVES IT WELL IN ITS NEW AVATAR AS A HOTEL
Following page 88: RELIGION AND ROYALTY MIX TOGETHER. A PROCESSION TAKES OUT AN IMAGE OF THE GODDESS

The royal *rasoda*, *jal khana* and *tambol khana* supplied food, drinking water and *pan supari* (betel and nuts) to the entire household. The king's personal kitchen only served his favourite wives, children and guests. Other queens, dowager queens and concubines had their separate kitchens. The royal cellars were well stocked with potent Rajasthani *asa* (fruit liqueurs) and raisin wines.

Aphrodisiacs were prepared by *vaids* in the City Palace *aushad khana* (dispensary). Other medicines were also made and stored there according to ancient ayurvedic, unani and Irani (indigenous healing systems) prescriptions. Sawai Jai Singh employed some Portuguese and French doctors, and had an interesting collection of European medical books. Since Ram Singh II's minority, British doctors started working on the king's staff.

The *mistry khana* (carpenters' workshop) made and repaired furniture for all the palaces. Modern European-style furniture came into fashion after 1840, and the City Palace is full of good reproductions.

The City Palace *farash khana* (storehouse) has some interesting Mughal and Rajasthani tents and pavilions. Man Singh's camping paraphernalia, which includes a beautiful double-storeyed *rawti* (durbar tent), stands out. Traditionally Jaipur's aristocracy could borrow *shamianas* (canopies), carpets, *durries* (rugs), palanquins, carriages and *howdahs* from the king during their family weddings.

chapter 8

Game for Festivals

Festivals brought out the best colours of royalty. During Dussehra, a fasting king worshipped Durga at Amber; at Diwali, he gave away gifts as dancing girls performed in Chandra Mahal; for Holi he rode on an elephant though the streets

CONTRADICTORY AS IT MAY SEEM, MOST MAHARAJAS were keen *shikaris* (hunters) and also good game wardens. They observed strict taboos about not killing the females of any four-legged species, and not killing at all during the breeding and rearing seasons. Tigers, panthers and leopards were selectively shot. Sometimes the Jaipur *shikar khana* records show only two tigers bagged by the viceroy or king, sometimes fifteen by various members of the royal family and their guests. Man-eaters and cattle-lifters had to be shot in public interest, and wild boars prevented from destroying the winter crops.

The hilly jungles around Jaipur were full of animals and birds because they were a royal preserve from medieval times. No one except the king, his sons, or special guests could hunt there right up to 1948. Black buck, cinkaras, wild boars, peacocks, partridges and rabbits could be seen very close to the city, especially around the lakes and other sources of water.

The Sawai Madhopur tiger shoots of the Jaipur rulers were famous in international circles. The royal family and their guests stayed at the quaint boat-shaped hunting lodge near Ranthambhor Fort. Tents were pitched on its grounds for the staff and *shikaris* to keep the show going.

The Sawai Madhopur Game Sanctuary has tigers, panthers, leopards, bears, lynx, wild boar, nilgai, sambhar, wolves, hyenas, cheetal, black buck, cinkara, black partridge, quails, green pigeons, wild fowl, peacocks and rabbits. The Chambal and Anas rivers have crocodiles, many varieties of fish, migratory teal, spot bills, mallards, pochards and bar-headed geese come to it in winter. Today Ranthambhor and Sawai Madhopur have become popular weekend haunts for wildlife lovers and conservationists.

When the jungles were a royal hunting preserve, *machans* (tree houses) were built for bagging tigers and panthers. Open jeeps were used to hunt wild boar, deer, partridge and rabbits. There were butts on most lakes for winter duck shoots.

Aodi Ram Sagar, or Ramgarh Bandha as it is popularly called, is an old Kachwaha fortress overlooking the main source of Jaipur's water supply. About twenty-five kilometres from the city, it also has a small shooting lodge modernised by Man Singh for his European and American guests. Old

snaps show Ram Singh II, Madho Singh II, their wives and families setting out for a day's hunt on elephants, horses and bullock chariots from Ramgarh, accompanied by hunters and beaters on foot. It was also a popular picnic spot providing boating, swimming and duck-shooting facilities, especially for the ladies who could not make the longer trips to Sawai Madhopur or Ranthambhor.

The religious festivals and feasts celebrated in royal Jaipur included Holi, Diwali, Dussehra, Teej, Gangaur, Basant Panchami, Ram Navami, Janamasthami, Maha Shiv Ratri, Guru Purnima, Raksha Bandhan, Sheetala Asthami, Bhanu Saptami and Makar Sankranti. These festivals not only broke the monotony of daily life, but also gave Jaipur's royalty, aristocracy and common folk the opportunity to meet, mingle and enjoy grand public spectacles, where feudal ties were renewed, and the state's wealth and prestige flaunted before visiting dignitaries and outsiders.

On major festivals, the king led the procession of elephants, horses, camels, and decorated *raths* (chariots) with his nobles, all dressed in traditional finery. Foot soldiers, musicians, and thousands of people followed, watched by large throngs of women and children.

Jaipur's Dussehra was really impressive. Dussehra is very special for the Rajputs because it is a combination of religious worship and military display. For nine days, Durga, Goddess of War, was worshipped by a fasting king with ritual prayers and goat sacrifices at Amber. On Vijaya Dashami, the tenth day, after an early morning *havan* (worship around a sacred fire), the king performed *shastra puja* (weapon worship) at the Chandra Mahal, assisted by his *raj purohit* (royal priest). Traditional purification rites and blessing of all arms, accoutrements and paraphernalia of royalty followed. Madho Singh II introduced the tradition of assembling the Jaipur state forces outside the city at Fateh Tibba. Here the state colours were taken down and re-hoisted with an artillery salute. Warriors honoured their arms and their mounts by anointing them with *kumkum* (vermilion) paste and rice, and by tying on them a protective red and white *mauli* (thread).

The Dussehra durbar is still held in the Diwan-i-aam, with several *sardars* and *seth sahukars* present, offering *nazar* (felicitation). (In the olden days the celebrations were far more elaborate.) At sunset, the king goes with his entourage, riding behind Sitaramji's icons enthroned on a six-horse chariot, to see the auspicious *neelkanth* (bluejay) being set free at Jai Pol. It is believed that seeing this bird, Lord Vishnu's mythological mount, is a lucky omen. The king then offers prayers to a *khejri* tree or *jhar* (bush), presents a coconut and a gold coin to the high priest of Galta Math, and returns to the City Palace. Bards would sing eulogies to Rama and his brother Lakshman in the past, whose victory over the demon-king Ravana, and the salvation of Rama's abducted wife, Sita, this ten-day-long festival commemorates.

Diwali, symbolising the Hindu new year, originated as a harvest festival. During this festival, prayers are offered to Lakshmi, goddess of wealth. The king worships the *Shri Yantra,* a magical wealth-endowing talisman, distributes sweets and gifts to the poor, and new clothes and monetary gifts to his relations, staff and family priests. Merchants and businessmen close old account books and open new ones on this day.

A time for merrymaking, feasting and visiting throughout India, in the royal Jaipur household, in olden days, Diwali began with dancing girls performing all day in the Chandra Mahal courtyard. The king wore a black and gold turban and black jacket to attend the Lakshmi Puja, which was performed by his seniormost queen. The royal ladies wore brand new *lehenga-odhni* (flared skirts and veil) costumes embroidered with gold and silver. For two nights, the entire city was illuminated by tiny earthenware lamps. The City Palace, Amber, Jaigarh, Nahargarh, Moti Doongri and Rambagh presented a grand spectacle when Diwali *diyas* (lamps) glittered, and fireworks exploded all over the city. The king always invited several family members and friends to celebrate Diwali, with a grand dinner followed by a gambling session for good luck, while the children set off crackers to welcome the Goddess of Wealth.

Until Maharaja Man Singh and Maharani Gayatri Devi moved out of Rambagh, Sharat Purnima (October full moon) was a major social event on the royal calendar. Selected guests—specially newlyweds—were invited to a formal dinner on the moonlit terrace. Chilled rice and milk *kheer* (rice pudding), full of dry fruits and raisins, topped with silver foil, was a speciality of this festival ushering in winter. Pink turbans and pink Rajasthani costumes were de rigueur on this light-hearted romantic occasion.

Holi is traditionally a rather rowdy but thoroughly enjoyable festival in royal Jaipur. This festival, which celebrates the harvest of

THE PRESENT MAHARAJA, BHAWANI SINGH, CELEBRATING HOLI, THE FESTIVAL OF COLOURS, IN JAIPUR. ROYALTY LESSENS ITS DISTANCE FROM THE HOI POLLOI, FREELY MIXING WITH THE CROWDS ON THE OCCASION
Preceding pages 90-91: THE RICH PALETTE OF RAJASTHANI LIFE PAINTS THE DESERT LANDSCAPE WITH A MYRIAD COLOURS WHENEVER THERE IS A FAIR

the winter crop, is the Indian version of the Mardi Gras, when liberties can be taken and social barriers ignored. All-male parties of *dhamal* singers and dancers gather in the palace courtyard, dancing to the mesmeric beat of a tambourine, saluting the king, singing special Holi songs, and putting daubs of red, pink, green and yellow *abheer* and *gulal* (coloured powder) on his face, hands and feet. The king rides on an elephant through the streets so that the people can indulge themselves by throwing coloured powder at him, or drenching him with coloured water from balconies and windows, shouting affectionate greetings, good-natured jibes and singing bawdy songs. Abandoning all decorum, men, women and children, high on sweetmeats and sherbat laced with *bhang* (marijuana), surround the king while he tries to keep them at a safe distance with his imported water hose and colour-stuffed wax pellets.

In the City Palace *zenana,* queens played Holi with friends, relations, and the wives of Jaipur's nobility. When the king, his sons, and brothers visited the royal ladies on Holi, they did their best to duck the menfolk in ornamental pools filled with coloured water. Everyone enjoyed the drenching, teasing, and the lavish lunch that followed.

Teej and Gangaur have always been festivals that are very special for the women of Rajasthan. A grand fair is held on Teej, and

Pages 94, 95: Polo is Man Singh II's legacy to Jaipur, where it is played not only on horseback but also on elephant-back. At one time the Raja had formed a team that won three British Open Championships
Following page 96: These City Palace retainers, (left) Siya Ram and (right) Mohd Surajuddin, are as much an attraction as the magnificent structure

married women are indulged with outdoor picnics, treats and gifts of henna, glass bangles and new clothes, which they proudly display while playing on the swings with their female friends and relations in mango groves and gardens to welcome the monsoon. Queens set the pace by visiting these gardens and taking the first swing. On Gangaur, Shiva's consort, Parvati, is traditionally worshipped in Rajasthan by maharanis led by virgin princesses. Elegantly dressed and bejewelled royal ladies circle the great Mother Goddess, offering flowers, green grass, lamps and incense. Unmarried girls pray for good husbands, married women for the health and long life of theirs. Folk songs liven the palace as lovely young Rajput girls wearing gold anklets and ivory bangles perform a dance known as the *ghoomar*, while the *dholans* (drummers) play their *dhol majeera* (long drums and cymbals).

The royal Gangaur statue symbolising the honour of the ruling house is then carried in procession under armed guard from the *zenani dyodhi* through the city. This is a hangover from Rajasthan's warlike past, when neighbours and enemies considered it a feat of arms to swoop down on a Gangaur procession, overcome its guardians, capture the statue, and carry it home to boast of their valour. Many Rajput blood feuds and vendettas originated at Gangaur festivals.

Today's Gangaur processions are more sedate. The elephant-borne statue escorted by dancing girls, musicians, and the colourfully-clad Maharaja and his kinsmen are taken to the Talkatora Lake, where several Gangaur statues belonging to the city's leading families are assembled. The Maharaja performs the ritual *puja* and the royal Gangaur bestows token gifts on all the assembled icons, 'takes the water', and is carried back to the City Palace, where it stays indoors for another year.

Before accession, there used to be a big Gangaur fair at Chaugan, with camel and horse races, food stalls, and pedlars selling colourful toys and trinkets. Jaipur's celebrated Naga sanyasis, a warlike ascetic sect, performed a sword dance as the grand finale, after which the Maharaja went to the Jai Niwas Garden. There, musicians and dancers entertained him while the royal ladies watched from secluded pavilions.

The Maharaja's birthday celebrations in Jaipur began with a nineteen-gun salute at sunrise, followed by his visit to Gobind Devji's temple, where the a *havan* (worship involving the lighting of a sacrificial fire) was performed and his horoscope for the coming year read. Alms were given to the poor and needy, and gifts to Brahmins. A formal military parade by the state forces was held, followed by an official birthday durbar in Sarbatta, when the chiefs, ministers and officials presented the king with their *nazar* (felicitation) in order of precedence. The Maharaja then met other visitors. In the afternoon, he attended the *zenana* durbar, over which his mother or the oldest dowager queen presided. The day was rounded off with a family luncheon and dinner party enlivened by music and dancing.

Today only Teej, Gangaur, Holi, Dussehra and Diwali are celebrated with the public participation of the present ex-Maharaja.

But royal Jaipur endures, fascinating visitors from all over the world. Though the basic mould of this 900-year-old kingdom's culture and society remained Rajasthani, Jaipur became the region's most progressive city because its Kachwaha rulers utilised Mughal and European ideas and innovations to improve their institutions and economy. Raja Man Singh in the sixteenth century, and Maharaja Sawai Man Singh II in the twentieth, used its proximity to Delhi with admirable foresight.

Their Jaipur has emerged as an unchallenged manufacturing-cum-marketing centre for all that is exotic and exquisite in Indian handcrafted collectors' items, specially gems and jewellery; carved semi-precious stones and silverware; enamelled objets d'art; miniature paintings and *pichwais* (wall hangings); *zari*, *zardozi* and sequin-work costumes, bags, slippers; marble statues, brassware; furnishing fabrics and fashionable garments.

A visual extravaganza, where the past surpasses the present, Jaipur seems to validate Einstein's theory of multilinear time. No wonder Rajasthan's dynamic capital has become one of the world's most popular destinations, promising a host of pleasurable and rewarding experiences. Even for visiting US presidents like Bill Clinton!